Revising The Agenda

Cycle A
Pentecost through Proper 17
Based on the Gospel Texts

William G. Carter

CSS Publishing Company, Inc
Lima, Ohio

REVISING THE AGENDA

FIRST EDITION

Copyright © 2019

by CSS Publishing Co., Inc.

Library of Congress Cataloging-in-Publication Data

Names: Carter, William G., 1960- author. Title: Revising the agenda : Cycle A Pentecost through Proper 17 based on the Gospel texts / William G. Carter. Description: First edition. I Lima, Ohio : CSS Publishing Company, Inc., [2019] Identifiers: LCCN 2019002493 I ISBN 9780788029851 (pbk. : alk. paper) I ISBN 0788029851 (pbk. : alk. paper) I ISBN 9780788029868 (ebk.) I ISBN 078802986X (ebk.) Subjects: LCSH: Bible. Matthew--Sermons. I Common lectionary (1992). Year A. I Pentecost--Sermons. I Church year sermons. I Sermons, American--21st century. Classification: LCC BS2575.54 .C37 2019 I DDC 252/.64--dc23

For more information about CSS Publishing Company resources, visit our website at www.csspub.com, email us at csr@csspub.com, or call (800) 241-4056.

e-book:
ISBN-13: 978-0-7880-2986-8
ISBN-10: 0-7880- 2986-X

ISBN-13: 978-0-7880-2985-1
ISBN-10: 0-7880-2985-1   Digitally Printed

*Dedicated to Guy Davis Griffith,
friend, pilgrim, brother on The Way.*

Introduction

Shortly after I was ordained as a minister, I attended a retreat for church leaders. The speaker was a seminary professor from a nearby state. He was not widely known in our circles, but spoke with a rare clarity that got right to the heart of pastoral ministry.

Over the course of three days, we prayed and sang together. We reflected on scripture and conversed about the challenges of maintaining a balanced life. We had a number of conversations with our speaker. His name was Neill Hamilton, and in the final session of the retreat, he spoke of why it was important for us to spend this kind of time together. "The church is God's mission to the world," he said, "but far too often, the world infects the church with the wrong kinds of values."

As he said to us, quoting one of his recent writings,

The reality is that the vast majority of persons in a typical congregation do not want themselves or their world to be transformed by the gospel. Instead, they want the minister to help them make life easier to manage while they and their world stay the same in every important respect.[1]

This was bracing truth. It felt as if we were being thrown into an icy lake to be baptized. After thirty years as a pastor, I can say he was exactly right.

The Christian life is a life of continuing conversion. Baptism may claim us as God's own beloved, but the children of God must grow up and mature. Jesus invites his followers to "Take my yoke upon you and learn from me" (Matthew 11:29). This is a life of ongoing transformation, not merely by our own effort, but by welcoming Christ's Spirit to make us more like him. In every sense, we are Christians who are still becoming Christians.

If there was a governing theme for the sermons, that seems to be it. Discipleship is a steady journey through the summer, when most of these lectionary texts are scheduled to be heard. Each text, like each sermon, is episodic. They proceed a step at a time. Yet each is an invitation to follow after Christ and to grow in grace. He is the one who revises our agenda, beckoning us repeatedly, "Come, follow me."

I offer these meditations on scripture as a resource for your spiritual journey. It's my privilege to share what I have heard the risen Christ whisper to me through study and prayer, in the grand hope that we might grow in faith, hope, and love.

My thanks are offered to the saints of First Presbyterian Church of Clarks Summit, PA, among whom I have served for many years. And I dedicate this volume to a great friend who has been my traveling companion for over three decades.

Contents

Day of Pentecost

John 20:19-23

From The Vantage Point Of Eternity

One Sunday after Easter, some children were playing in a Sunday school room. The class was about to start. The teacher was pulling together a few things for the lesson, and he heard them playing over in the corner. They had built a small wall out of cardboard bricks, and one of them was hiding down behind it.

Apparently the little guy was playing the role of Jesus after Easter, which he must have heard about in a worship service. He called out, "Hey Pontius Pilate, I'm back."

The kid who was playing Pilate said, "Where are you? I don't see you." The first kid giggled. Then suddenly he jumped up, kicked over the wall, and started throwing the bricks at his opponent. The teacher had to separate them, noting later that this was an impressive way to begin the class.

Perhaps the truly impressive truth is that there is no story like that in the Bible. Did you ever notice what the Bible does *not* say? When Jesus came back from the dead, he never retaliated against those who put him in the tomb. To die as he died, to be humiliated as he was humiliated, yet he never spoke a harsh word against his enemies.

When Jesus returned from the dead, he did not confront Pontius Pilate for ordering his execution. He did not return to frighten the soldiers who laughed as they drove nails through his wrists. Jesus did not go to the temple to condemn the priests who first condemned him. And when he appeared on Easter evening to the very disciples who abandoned him, he said, "Peace to you." Then he breathed on them and said, "Receive the Holy Spirit."

It was a remarkable moment. They were huddled in a locked room. They were afraid, even though his last words to them were, "Let not your hearts be troubled." They were divided and suspicious, even though Jesus' final prayer was for them "to be one." Simon Peter was there, even though he was named as the violent swordsman who cut off the ear of the high priest's servant. Yet Jesus appeared and he did not blame or condemn anybody. Instead he said a second time, "Peace to you."

The scholar Raymond Brown said this is not a wish for peace, but a declaration that peace is now within the room.[2] The Greek text is a statement of fact: Jesus was making good on his statement, "Peace, I leave with you. My peace I give to you." The risen Christ does not carry a grudge. He took away the sin of the world, lifting the poison from the earth and onto his cross. And he came to say, "Peace is in the room."

The larger point is that something had changed in the world. In the cross and resurrection of Jesus, something had been accomplished. Something had been "finished."

In chapter after chapter of his book, John gave us glimpses of something holy breaking through the ordinary moments of life: at a wedding bash water is turned into wine, a multitude is fed in a deserted place, a paralyzed man is healed after years of lingering around the miracle shrine. Now Christ breaks into a locked room to pronounce peace where there was fear. He declares forgiveness where there has been disappointment. This is a glimpse of the eternal life of God where there is peace and forgiveness. If we can receive the peace and forgiveness, God offers the Pentecost power to change what we do and how we live.

Some years ago, a great theology teacher passed away. His name was Shirley Guthrie, and he taught at Columbia Theological Seminary near Atlanta. When his end was near, the seminary president reported of one of her last conversations with Dr. Guthrie. She said they were talking about his impending death, and she observed how he seemed to be at peace. With that, she said, his eyes twinkled and with amazement in his voice he said, "Yes, and the peace is bigger than I imagined. "She notes, he went on to say that he had quit worrying about all the things he had to do ... *ought* to do. He said, "It turns out these things are not as important to God as I thought. It's all about forgiveness."[3]

That is a wonderful testimony about what is most important. All our unfinished business will not matter in God's eternity. The squabbles within our families will not amount to much after we are gone. A lot of the personal grudges that burden us today will not mean very much in five hundred years. In fact, most of the great issues that divide the world and threaten the church are not issues that our great-grandchildren are going to care much about. If they will go to a church, what they will want to know is if Jesus Christ reveals the grace and truth of God.

The risen Christ returns to the church to speak of peace. In his death and resurrection, he has accomplished peace between heaven and earth. That means forgiveness is possible. Forgiveness will always be possible, because

Jesus Christ is alive. He is eternally alive, and he speaks to us of what it means to live here and now in the life of God's eternity. It's all about forgiveness.

To get the movement of redemption started, he speaks a word to the church: "If you forgive the sins of any, they are forgiven them; if you retain the sins of any, they are retained." The Greek word for "forgive" is cancel. The Greek word for "retain" is clutch. That's the eternal choice: are you going to cancel or clutch? Are you going to let go or hang on? Sadly, some of the people who struggle the most with this choice are church people.

I subscribe to a weekly magazine, and was delighted to discover the editor had written a wonderful piece on the power of forgiveness. The editor is a friend, so I went online to the magazine website and wrote a quick note of thanks. "Your work is consistently helpful," I said, "and I really appreciated the article."

No more than twenty minutes later, I received a piece of hate mail. A minister in West Virginia had read my two-sentence note online and fired back his artillery at me. With a barrage of angry words, he called my friend a hack, told me how he has ruined the magazine, and said in no uncertain terms that I was wrong to give him a compliment, because it's people like him who are destroying our church. Then he added a few surreal words: "And have a happy Easter."

I have received some unusual mail over the years. If it's signed, it goes into a file. If it's unsigned, it goes into the circular file. This note was really unusual, because it was the first time I was ever condemned for complimenting somebody for an article on forgiveness... and the writer was a minister. Obviously he was clutching something that he did not want to let go.

What should we do? Forgive or retain? Cancel or clutch? For my part I decided to cancel; I looked at that nasty e-mail and hit the word "delete." My prayer was that God would lighten the writer's heart so he could release his grip on my friend. As somebody once said, "When you forgive, you set a prisoner free. And then you discover that the prisoner was you."[4]

Jesus did not hold a grudge against Pontius Pilate. He did not accuse the twelve disciples. Neither did Jesus act with spiritual smugness to announce he was sufficiently superior enough to forgive. He simply let go of what he could have chosen to hold. Twice he said to his frightened disciples "peace to you," and he said it before they could even apologize for what they did or what they neglected to do. He spoke from the wisdom of God's eternity. The sin of the world is taken away for those who let it be taken away.

In the Bible translation called *The Message*, Eugene Peterson offers a helpful translation of these words of Jesus: "If you forgive someone's sins, they're gone for good. If you don't forgive sins, what are you going to do with them?" (John 20:23)

Isn't that the choice? You can cancel somebody's sins and let go of them. Or you can clutch them, hold onto them, keep a list of them, and imagine punishment for all of them. In the immortal line that Fred Craddock once ascribed to the resentful soul, "Every morning you can go out back and lift the rock just to make sure the snake is still there."[5]

The Pentecost power that Christ gives to the church is the power to forgive. In Christ, God forgives. In the church, Christ sends the church to forgive as the Father has sent him. He breathes on us and says, "Receive my Spirit." He gives us the power to continue what he has begun – and by giving us his Spirit, he declares all of us can be his priests. That's what priests do: their primary job is to absolve people of their sins.

It really comes down to this: either you are a priest or you are a victim. Those are the only two options. We can let the hurt go or save it to use later. If we are priests, we can free others of shame and our own souls of hurt. If we are victims, we hold onto the hurt, which is like holding onto a virus.

If the hurts consume us, it will be hard to be the priest. We will wonder if we can ever give up the overwhelming pain. But the truth of Pentecost is that we have some help with this. Jesus breathed the Holy Spirit upon us before he called us to forgive. The Spirit gives us the courage to do the work of Jesus Christ.

As someone said, "What this means is that we disciples are not called to produce forgiveness. We're called to be the priest pronouncing that which has been produced on the cross. We're called to open the locks and throw open the door, and walk back into the world as a priest who is unafraid. The only alternative is to live in shrinking prisons of hurt."[6]

What did Jesus announce on the cross? He said, "It is finished." Either it is finished or it isn't. Either all sins are forgiven or Christ died for nothing. Either Christ is alive or we are all still imprisoned by our hurts. Either the world is ruled by punishment, or the power of Pentecost is among us, waiting to be practiced.

"Receive the Holy Spirit," he said. Then he breathed on them.

Trinity Sunday

Matthew 28:16-20

Converts Or Disciples?

Whatever else we want to say about this story, it is an Easter story. At dawn on the day he was raised, the risen Christ said, "Tell my brothers to go to Galilee." When they did, they saw him, just as he promised.

Our text is the only Galilee appearance that Matthew reported. It sounds like other Easter stories. Christ is present ... and the disciples have mixed feelings. As Matthew noted, "When they saw him, they worshiped him, and some doubted." It's like every Easter Sunday, for it's a mixed house. Have you ever noticed? Even when we blow the Easter trumpets, some of the people present are scratching their heads.

There is also a pathetic note about the little church. Perhaps you noticed in the reading how many disciples were left: eleven! The church is shrinking. Easter does not increase the actual number of believers. If anything, it reveals who the true believers are. There used to be twelve, but Judas fell away. Now there are eleven. Among these eleven, some worship and some doubt; I will bet for a few of them, it was a good dose of both.

Then Jesus gave his commission to his church. He told them what he wanted them to do, after he said a word about himself. "All authority has been given to me," he said. He had the authority of heaven, the authority of earth. In speaking of Jesus Christ, authority is one of Matthew's favorite words. "Exousia" is the word in Greek – "authority" – and Jesus had received it from God.

The devil had offered him authority in the desert. He took Jesus to a very high mountain, extended his arms, and said, "Look at all the nations of the world and their splendor. Wouldn't you like to have all of that? Just say the word and it can be yours." But Jesus told him to go back to hell. What the devil had offered him was a crown without a cross. He made some bogus promise that Jesus could have world dominion if he skipped the resistance, the arrest, the suffering, the crucifixion, the waiting on God. There would be no crown without a cross.

On the other side of the tomb, there is authority. All authority of heaven and earth, given to the crucified and risen Lord. This is an Easter story.

Jesus was risen for the benefit of the world, for the whole world. I don't know if you remember this about Matthew, but he was quite specific to say that Jesus had once confined his ministry to fellow Jews. He taught the Jews, he healed the Jews, and that was it. Once he approached by a woman of different nationality who begged him to heal her daughter. He ignored her, but she insisted. He said, "Sorry, lady, I was sent only to the lost sheep of Israel (15:24). That is my scope, my limitation."

Before, when he sent out his followers to do ministry, Jesus limited where they could go. "Don't go among any Gentiles," he said, "but go rather to the lost sheep of the house of Israel" (10:6). Christian faith began as Jewish faith – Jesus the Jew went only to the Jews. He was the Messiah for people who wanted a Messiah, provided he was the kind of Messiah that they wanted.

But now it was after Easter. Easter changed everything. Jesus had taught in Israel, but now his instruction is intended for all. He had healed those in his neighborhood, but now he was available for the healing of all people. Any self-imposed restrictions were lifted. He had all authority, in heaven and on earth. So he sent his people to "all nations." Indeed Christ said, "all nations."

We call this the great commission. For the better part of 150 years, we have been clear about what this means. This brief story is the favorite of mission committees in all kinds of the church. It pushes us beyond parochialism to take the gospel to every people in every land.

In the history books of the church, we learn about a man named Samson Occom. He was a Native American. In 1759, the Presbyterian Church ordained him as a minister, the first Native American minister. He was a member of the Mohegan nation and sent as a missionary to the Native Americans. On the day of his ordination, the preacher based his sermon on our Bible passage.[7] The message was clear: "White people like us have given a Native American like you something you did not have, and we want you to give it away to as many of your people as you can." Church leaders promised him a good salary, the same salary as the white preachers, but the money never showed up and he lived in deep poverty for most of his life.

Yet he went out to preach, because he was a Christian. And being a Presbyterian, he went out to begin a school. It was a school for poor Native Americans, to teach them to read, write, and to love God. A friend took him to England for an eighteen-month preaching tour, and the

Reverend Samson Occom raised a lot of money for the sake of education. He was a convincing preacher. Even King George III made a personal donation.

When he returned to the American colonies, Samson Occom discovered his benefactor had lied to him. He had neglected to care as promised for Occom's wife and children, who were now destitute. Not only that, the funds Occom had raised were redirected toward establishing Dartmouth College for white people, rather than to educate his beloved Native Americans.

That's the kind of story that makes you wonder if there are any Christians within the church. Sadly it is not the only tale of good-hearted missionary efforts gone awry. The risen Christ sends us to every nation on his behalf. We are his hands, his feet, his voice, his heart. Yet if you know the history, our efforts have been mixed at best. There are many sad stories of European Christians who spoke to people who were neither European nor Christian. They tried to make other people Christians, but inevitably tainted them as Europeans. Sometimes it was conversion by coercion. These days it may be conversion by consumerism and consumption.

Perhaps the most telling indicator comes from the Korean church, which the American Presbyterians nurtured. There are far more Korean Presbyterians now than there are American Presbyterians, and the Korean church is sending missionaries to us. As one of them said to me, "It must be so difficult to be a Christian in America; you have so many riches and your people have become so selfish. So few Americans seem to pay any attention to God in any meaningful way."

Are there any Christians within the church? That seems to lie at the heart of Christ's great commission. He did not charge his people to make converts, but to make disciples. Alongside any intention to grow the church in numbers is a greater concern to grow the church in depth. A disciple is a student of Jesus. Disciples have a relationship that is growing, and learning, and serving. There is something more at work in them than merely taking up space in a pew. They work hard to understand what the gospel is all about. They struggle to bring those Christian insights to bear on the places where they work and the ways they spend their time and money. And it's a lifelong process.

In recent years, the best minds of the church have pointed out that we can't simply coast along and become "automatically Christian." We have to work at it with intentionality. I think of the work of Douglas John Hall who taught theology in Toronto. "It used to be," said Hall, "that somebody could pick up Christian odors in the air, and that would be enough to shape their lives. These days, according to the research, white Westerners cease to be Christian at a rate of 7,600 per day."[8] For us to be Christian, in this day and age, will take something more merely than having our names on a list on a church office computer. Being a disciple is more than being a church member.

"Go and make disciples of all nations," says Jesus. I think that includes making disciples in this nation as much as it means making disciples in any other nation. This is more than a Mission Committee text; it is a Christian Education Committee text. A serving church is a learning church; a church that grows in its love for Jesus is a church that grows in its love for its neighborhood; it all goes hand in hand.

The clue for all of this is the place where the Easter Jesus met his disciples. Do you remember from our text where that was? They went to Galilee, "to the mountain where he directed them." What mountain? Anybody want to guess? It's the mountain where we have been before – the Sermon on the Mount mountain. After Easter, he directed them back to the place where he gathered them together and began to teach. The Easter Christ continued to instruct us, saying,

- Blessed are the poor in spirit, for theirs is the kingdom of heaven.
- You are the salt of the earth.
- Love your enemies.
- Be complete as your heavenly Father is complete.
- Do not store up treasures on earth.
- Seek first the kingdom of God.
- Enter through the narrow gate.
- The good person brings good things out of a good treasure.
- Whoever gives a cup of cold water to these little ones will not lose their reward.
- Humble yourself like a little child.
- Pick up your cross and follow me.
- Forgive one another seventy times seven.
- Just as you did it to the least of these, you did it to me.

This is where disciples are made: by sitting at the feet of the teacher. He said to those who are baptized, "You have to learn everything I have commanded you. And then you have to live everything I have taught." This is his commission, and it's going to take us a lifetime of constant effort to get it right.

If we think for a minute that we can slack off, he gave us a blessing that was also a warning. He said, "Remember, I am with you to the end of the age." I am right here, in the middle of your circle. I am right here, hidden in word and sacrament. I am with you in the love that you share and the concern that you visibly offer to one another. I am with you until you grow into the fullness of what it means to love God and neighbor. I am with you until you fully discover just how much God loves the world.

He is with us, just as the angel promised at Christmas. Just as he himself declared after Easter, Jesus Christ is with us. His continuing work is to make us into the kind of people who share God's love and justice with every person under heaven, to the point that they, too, will share that love and justice with others. That, if you ask me, is the meaning and the promise of the Great Commission.

How Much Should We Pack?

As much as I like to travel, I am never sure how much to pack. When my wife and I take off for a week long vacation, we do our best to keep a week's worth of possessions down to one suitcase. That is the goal. There is never a guarantee it will happen.

Packing is determined by two contradictory principles: how do we move quickly? How can we be prepared for every contingency? How many pairs of pants can I take, or in my wife's case, how many pairs of shoes? Should we pack a sweatshirt? Does it rain in New Mexico? How about a suit jacket, in case our hosts take us out to dinner? And given that we booked a very small rental car, will the suitcase fit in the back?

Packing is an art form. There are experts throughout the internet, suggesting "How to pack like a Ninja." They offer great advice: roll up your t-shirts and take one less than you think you will need. Roll up your socks and stick them in your shoes. To save space, wear a jacket onto the plane. Never waste valuable suitcase space.

On the other hand, it is possible to forget the essentials. Like the kid who was in such a hurry to get out of the house and spend a Friday night with friends. Around eleven that night, there was a phone call. A sheepish voice whispered, "Dad, could you bring over some underwear?

I forgot to bring some. But whatever you do, don't tell my friends." Of course I didn't tell her friends; I saved that story for a sermon.

So I was paying close attention in this text when Jesus sent out twelve of his followers. He gave them the authority to do his work and sent them out to travel around as he has been traveling around. And what was the best advice at the heart of his commission? Don't take anything with you.

In Eugene Peterson's translation, Jesus said, "Go to the lost, confused people right here in the neighborhood... Bring health to the sick. Raise the dead. Touch the untouchables. Kick out the demons. You have been treated generously, so live generously... travel light."[9]

We know that too much baggage can get in the way. That was our discovery during a family trip years ago. On the way through the Mojave Desert, our rental car got a flat tire about a hundred miles shy of Barstow, California. The tire was changed with a spare, but the punctured tire wouldn't fit underneath where the spare came from. And there was no room for the tire <u>inside</u> the car because there was too much luggage, so it had to go on somebody's lap.

"Travel light" is good advice. Yet Jesus pushed it to extremes: "Carry no bag for your journey. Take no sandals, no walking stick. Forget about an extra shirt. And most of all, take no money."

That reminds me of the hazing story when my father joined a college fraternity. They blindfolded him late one night and put him in the trunk of a car. Then they drove around for 45 minutes, stopped somewhere, and told him to get out. He had no wallet, no money, no compass, no flashlight. The boys said, "See you back at the fraternity house. Figure out how you're going to get there," and sped away.

Obviously he made it back or I wouldn't be telling the story. He never explained how he did it, but he did say it wasn't easy.

Jesus was not hazing anybody. He was sending them out to do ministry. He had been healing a lot of people and there was more work to do than he could get done. A human being can only put in so many eighteen-hour days, can only be in one place at a time. So he called out twelve of his followers to extend the work. Jesus gave them direction, commissioned them to go, and said, "Don't pack anything."

Well, that did not mean that he wouldn't give them anything. You know what he gave them? The same thing he gives to us: a small sack of words. Jesus said, "When you go somewhere, say, 'The kingdom of God has come near to you.' That is, God is ruling over heaven and earth, and God is right here. And the second thing you say is 'Peace be to this house!' That's what I give you. That is all you must carry. Nothing else is necessary. You are sent into the world with a handful of words."

In a way, that is a relief. The words Jesus gave are simple words. They are easy to remember, not too heavy to carry. It is good to know that God's work can be done without a lot of props. We need no bag, no sandals, no purse. We need no flip-charts, no brochures, no PowerPoint presentations. That is refreshing because the props can get in the way.

Years ago, when my sister worked at a summer church camp, she brought back a collection of short passages that the staff used for devotions. It was a snarky little collection of wisecracking little parables, which is probably why I kept it still on my shelf. Here's one of my favorites:

In a certain town, an advertising executive decided to sell God. She invited some clients to a presentation. Then she got busy. First she converted the "God message" to a variety of abstract images projected onto a screen. Next she added a catchy soundtrack with guitars and drums. Finally she hired a caterer to serve drinks and hors d'oeuvres in the softly-lit room. As her clients arrived, she chatted with them casually. Then came the visual pitch. Afterward people complimented her creative approach. She was pleased and said she was glad they liked it. With a chuckle she added, "I hope you'll buy my product." People looked confused and uncomfortable. Finally someone said, "Oh, are you selling something?"[10]

The props can get in the way. Contrast that to what writer Frederick Buechner reminded us about Alcoholics Anonymous. The group meets in church basements and community rooms because an addiction to alcohol has damaged their lives. They have no budget, no leadership hierarchy, and no facility to call their own. The agenda is to tell their own stories, acknowledge where they made mistakes, share how they try to straighten out their lives, and to talk about how they pursue the courage to keep going.

"Isn't that what church was meant to be?" Buechner asks: "Sinners Anonymous."[11]

"I send you without a bag or sandals or purse," said Jesus, for God's work is best done with words. At the bottom of it all, we need no steeple, no pulpit, no organ, no blackboard, no office. In fact, we don't even need a coffee pot. Don't get me wrong; these things are nice, but in the ultimate economy of God, all we are given are a few words. It is refreshing.

What delights me even more is that Jesus suggests our words can carry the freight of the gospel. I had forgotten that words have such power. Of course, not just any words will do. Jesus gives us the right kind of words. He gives us words of blessing and words of truth.

Whenever you go into a house, said Jesus, say a blessing. Say "Peace be to this house!" It makes no demand. It requires no decision. It simply announces the salvation that Jesus came to bring. As someone puts it, "When you speak like that, you release God's good news into the air. God offers peace to all within hearing. Anyone hungering for such wholeness is free to respond on their own terms.[12]

When you go into a town, said Jesus, tell people the truth. You can eat with people and heal the sick. You can paint their houses and mow their lawns. But don't forget to speak up and say, "God's kingdom has come near to you." You see, that's the truth! Regardless of how effective your good deeds, regardless of whether or not anybody wants you around, you need to speak up and say, "God's kingdom has come near to you."

For we serve God's kingdom, not yours, mine, or theirs. The kingdom's arrival does not depend on you or me. The kingdom is at hand, regardless of how many good deeds we do along the way. God's reign has broken into human history. So we speak up and say so. Announce that God is here, that new possibilities for life are at hand.

It encourages me to hear such good news, especially given our circumstances. The world is not knocking down our door to hear the gospel. This morning's newspaper reports there is just as much pain and suffering as there was yesterday. That is all the more reason for Jesus to send us out into the world. He allows us no bag, no sandals, no purse, and no props. He sends us out as lambs in the midst of wolves, carrying only a few fragile words. Still the question remains: Are words enough? Do they have sufficient power? Is there anything we can say in God's name to make a tangible difference in a painful world? What do you think?

Walt Wangerin, the Lutheran storyteller, told about his church organist, an imposing woman named Joselyn Fields. At 47, she was stricken with cancer. Every season of the year, he went out to visit the woman.

He didn't know what to say, nor did he understand what he had the right to say. He wore out the psalms, because they seemed safe. He prayed that the Lord's will be done, but was too frightened to tell either the Lord or Joselyn what the Lord's will ought to be. By his own estimation, he bumbled.

One day after she awoke from surgery, he decided to be cheerful, to enliven her and to avoid the specter that unsettled him -- the death. He chattered. He spoke brightly of the sunlight outside, and vigorously of the tennis he had played that morning, sweetly of the flowers, hopefully of the day she would sit again at the organ, reading music during his sermon. But Joselyn rolled a black eye his way. She raised one bony finger to his face and said, "Shut up." He did, and he kept visiting her.

Her health did not improve. The young pastor kept visiting, only to discover he was attending her decline. He did not know what to say. The words didn't come. One afternoon, in particular, he entered the room and sat in silence. She looked at him and said nothing in return. As evening came, the Holy Spirit descended on the room, bringing the most appropriate words.

Walt says he turned to Joselyn, opened his mouth, and said, "I love you." Joselyn opened her eyes and put out her arms. She hugged him. He says poignantly

> "I hugged those dying bones. She whispered,
> `I love you, too.' That was all we said. But that
> was the power from on high, cloaking both of us
> in astonished simplicity, even as Jesus had said it
> would."[13]

When she died, Walt said the grief was bearable, for death had already lost its grip.

"Behold," Jesus said, "I send you into the world to do my work. You don't need a fat purse, or a bag, or brand new sandals." All he gives us are a handful of words. Words of blessing: "Peace be with you!" Words of truth: "God is ruling, and close at hand."

Above all else, he gives us words of love. That is what we need. They are enough.

Proper 7 / Ordinary Time 12

Matthew 10:24-39

Division Of The House

The more we read the Bible, the more we see things we might wish Jesus never said. This passage is one of them: "Do not think that I have come to bring peace to the earth; I have not come to bring peace, but a sword." Did any of us come to church today to hear him say that?

This is the season for family reunions. Most of us have been in gatherings that include fathers, mothers, grandparents, and children. It it is somewhat disturbing to come to church today and hear Jesus say, "I have come to set a man against his father."

I recall a big family wedding. The highlight for one father was not hearing the vows, throwing the birdseed, or eating a slice of cake. It was watching his four-year-old girl walk down the aisle in a white dress. This time she was only the flower girl, but you can guess what he was thinking. There may be a day in twenty years when she walks down the aisle in another white dress, this time with Daddy on her arm. When the scriptures are opened today, the words are stunning, for Jesus says, "Whoever loves his daughter more than me is not worthy of me."

It sounds like Jesus was standing against the family. A lot of us don't want to hear that. We want the church to encourage family members to get along, to bring people closer together especially if they live under the same roof, and to be an advocate for unity not division. Yet Jesus said the very purpose of his mission was not to stop family fights, but to start them.

We can look at the context, but the context does not help. After all, Jesus was giving marching orders to the first twelve missionaries. He gathered an odd and diverse group of people together and prepared them to go into the world. His training began with a scattering of advice:

- Don't pack a lot of unnecessary props. The word you bear is sufficient (10:5-15).
- Don't worry about what to say. The word will be given to you (10:16-23)
- Don't inflate your opinion of yourselves. You are servants, not masters. Remember that (10:24-25).
- Don't be afraid of what people will say about you or what they do to you. In God's good time, every dark secret will be exposed (10:26-28).
- Don't count yourselves as worthless, either, for God holds you in such high esteem that even the hairs on your head are numbered (10:29-31).
- Don't deny me and I won't deny you. Keep your faith and I will keep you (10:32-33).

These are helpful things to hear. We keep marching along until we stumble over verse 34. "Do not think that I have come to bring peace to the earth; I have not come to bring peace. I have come to bring a sword." I confess that I have spent most of this week trying to find a way to swallow these words, but it virtually impossible without causing indigestion.

For instance, Jesus spoke only of man against father, daughter against mother, and perhaps most logically, daughter-in-law against mother-in-law. It is a short list, suggesting generations turning against one another. By contrast, he did not speak of husband against wife, at least not in Matthew. He said that in the gospel of Luke, but not here.

No, Jesus drew from a list in the writings of the prophet Micah (Micah 7:5-7). He pointed to a division between generations: children against parents, and parents against children. The prophet declared one generation should stand against another. Your enemies shall live in your own house. The gospel clarification is that the cause of this conflict is Jesus Christ our Lord.

If this is true, we may have to throw away next year's Christmas cards, the likes of which we bought on sale during the week before New Year's Day. You know the cards. They portray blue angels singing about peace on earth and joy to the world. Those cards may have to get tossed out, because peace and joy are only one part of the Christmas story.

There is another part, too. After the baby Jesus was born, his mother took him to the temple. She wanted to present him before God, just as the good book told her to do. While she was there, an old man named Simeon shuffled up to her. He peeked into that blue blanket and praised the Lord for what he saw. But then he said something else. "This child is destined for the rising and falling of many, and Mary, because of this child, a sword will pierce your own soul too" (Luke 2:25 –35).

In Matthew's account of Christmas, wise men from the east appeared to ask, "Where is the newborn king?" With that, the incumbent king sent out his swordsmen to eliminate all the newborn children who could possibly be a threat to him.(Matthew 2: 1-16) The birth of Christ set that into motion.

Jesus was born into this world and his own family was not exempt from the sword. If anybody should have had a happy home life, it should have been Jesus. If anybody should have lived to a ripe old life with his parents, it should have been the Lord. But that is not how the story goes, and that is not what he expected;

Jesus said, "Do not think that I have come to bring peace to the earth. I have not come to bring peace. I have come to bring a sword."

The more these words sink in, the more I think to myself: how did he know? Our world has been visited by the Son of God. The stunning response is that his visit has created all kinds of problems. Just when we were touched by grace, sin grabbed hold and didn't let go. Just when we saw glimpses of unity, division disrupted our better intentions. Just when we thought we knew the way beyond hatred, a sword started swinging.

How did Jesus know? How did he know that, in the year 1850, 46 members of the Presbyterian church in Owego, New York, would split off to form their own church down the street. It seems that one Sunday morning the Presbyterian minister dared to pray for African American slaves. Many church members got upset about that and censured the minister. Then, in turn, these 46 members got upset with the people who had gotten upset with the minister. In the name of Christ they left. They began a Congregational church one block away.[14]

How did Jesus know? How did he know a church would be burned to the ground in Charlotte, North Carolina? It was such a pretty building, full of warm and joyful people. The congregation was steeped in history. It was created as a Christian fellowship for freed African American slaves. One night, a teenager with white skin crept through the shadows to set the building on fire. She could not tolerate the possibility of fellow Christians singing and rejoicing if they didn't look like her.[15]

How did Jesus know? How did he know that the people who follow him could leap at one another's throats? If you bring two or three Christians together, you might have five or six different opinions. If you study a difficult topic in light of our faith, tempers can flare and voices will raise. If you identify an issue to address, work toward a consensus, till some common ground, and find a shared vocabulary, someone will certainly wag a finger and say, "You're wrong."

Wisdom may tell us that people of good faith often differ, yet a warlike impulse within us will not settle for that. We prefer to choose up sides, draw lines in the sand, and affirm our own correctness. We want to pick up our own swords rather than carry the cross given to us. As a seasoned minister once said, "The heretic might not be the person who gets burned at the stake; but you can always bet that the heretic is always the person who fans the fire."

So maybe we can begin to understand why Jesus had to say, "Do not think that I have come to bring peace to the earth; I have not come to bring peace; I have come to bring a sword." He knew the best way to create dissention, difficulty, and strife was to start loving everybody. Yet he kept loving. He understood that the quickest way to disturb a close group of friends was to invite an outsider to join them for supper. Yet he kept inviting. He realized the fastest way to divide a house was to treat everybody fairly, to consider everybody equally, to forgive everybody without any desire to get even or to keep score. Yet that was the cross he chose to carry. And this is the cross he hands over to us.

He taught them, saying, "Love your neighbor. Do not judge. Go an extra mile. Make peace with your accuser." In response, a large crowd of thugs came out against him with clubs and swords.

One of his own disciples pulled out a sword and came out swinging. Jesus said, "Put your sword back; for all who take the sword will perish by the sword." Somebody said, "But Jesus, you said it yourself: you came to bring a sword."

Well, it's a different kind of sword than we might think. We would do well to regard a picture from the early church, a portrait of Jesus from the book of Revelation. His hair is pure white, as a sign of holiness. His eyes are like fire, as a symbol of love. In his hand he holds seven stars, as a sign of authority. From his mouth comes a sharp, two-edged sword.(Revelation 1:12-16)

This is a dramatic portrayal of the truth that the sword Jesus brought is the word that Jesus spoke. When he spoke, he made a difference. When the Christ still speaks, his word cuts through.

I cannot speak for you, but I confess that I'm not always sure I want him to speak. I might have to change who I am. I would have to confront my own unfinished business. I know all too well the unredeemed corners of my life. I have an elaborate defense system that protects me from every unwelcome intrusion. Truth be told, I don't allow God to get that close ... even though the one thing I want more than anything else is for God to get that close.

"I have come to bring a sword," he said. Try as I might, I cannot defend myself against those words. I can only respond to them, and it is clear what that would mean.

- With a word of truth, the Lord cuts away all in our lives that is false.
- With a word of health, the Savior separates us from all in our lives that is diseased.
- With a word that demands a life or death commitment, Christ trims away every lazy allegiance, every partial affirmation, every half-hearted hope.

As one New Testament writer put it, "Indeed, the word of God is living and active, sharper than any two-edged sword, piercing until it divides soul from spirit, joints from marrow; it is able to judge the thoughts and intentions of the heart. And before God no creature is hidden, but all are naked and laid bare to the eyes of the one to whom we must render an account."(Hebrews 4:12-13)

Do we really want to be exposed like that? Can we let the risen Lord cut that close? Are we willing to let a living God make a difference in our lives? Are we willing to love Jesus more than anything or anybody? Am I willing to trust him enough that I would lose my life for his sake?

If our faith is real and alive, these are the questions that never go away. They never go away. Even if we believe we have answered the questions before, they never go away, because they bring us into the presence of a God who accepts us as we are, yet who loves us enough to change us into a totally new creation.

All it takes is a simple "yes" and a laying down of arms. Then the transformation can begin.

I cannot predict how it will go. Nobody can expect the transformation will be easy. But there is one thing that I know for certain: when the Lord begins to work in our lives, the place where he always begins is the place closest to home.

Welcoming Jesus

Some years ago, my wife and I landed on the mystical island of Iona. Located off the western coast of Scotland, the small island has an abbey that traces its roots back to the sixth century. The abbey has been rebuilt over the last eighty years, and it now serves as a center for conferences and spiritual retreats.

We arrived on an August afternoon in time for the evening worship service. Taking our seats in the ancient stone sanctuary, we discovered we were in the midst of a Christian youth conference. There were people in their teens and early twenties who gathered there from across Europe, and they had planned the vespers.

"We welcome you in the name of Jesus the Christ," said the youthful leader. She announced the theme of the worship service was hospitality. "But rather than make this a theoretical concept," she said, "we would like you to stand up, find somebody that you do not know, and go sit with that person through the rest of the service." To my astonishment, everybody did.

By contrast, on a sparsely populated winter Sunday in my own congregation, I can't get people to move three rows forward, much less sit with people they do not know. I have invited, begged, cajoled, even bargained to shorten the sermon, but with no result. Folks settle back, fasten the invisible seatbelts in their favorite pews, and fold their arms, as if to say, "You're never going to get me to move."

But here was the miracle on a mystical Scottish island: people got up, introduced themselves to strangers they had never met, and then moved somewhere else to sit together for the rest of a worship service. Can you possibly imagine something like that? It was a miracle, a miracle of Christian hospitality.

I wondered why this must be a miracle, and not a regular practice. Perhaps if we worship in a church on a regular basis, we begin to stake out a place we can call our own. Maybe we like the freedom of sitting near an aisle, or the comfort of dwelling within the pack. If we perceive ourselves to be outsiders or even observers, we might sit near the back. If we aren't concerned with what anybody thinks of us, maybe we march down front where we sing as loudly as we want.

Recently I met with the leaders of a congregation where there will be a change in pastoral leadership. As we were getting acquainted, one of the elderly women reminded everybody that she had a favorite pew. "Not only that," she said, "it's my pew, because it was my mother's pew. Even though she's been long gone, it feels like she is still here somehow as long as I can sit in my own family pew." Curiously enough, or perhaps not so curiously, her congregation has only about a dozen people sitting in any of the pews these days. There is no credible threat that anybody will ever steal her seat, but there is the real possibility that, unchecked, her congregation could implode and disappear.

This is a sermon about hospitality. Hospitality is the opposite of guarding your own turf. Hospitality is making room for others. As the spiritual teacher Henri Nouwen said so well, hospitality is "the creation of a free space where the stranger can enter and become a friend instead of an enemy."[16] To be hospitable is to create that space, to make room for strangers. It is an intentional act of welcome, not merely a concept we think about but an act that we do.

Pause for a minute and remember the last time when somebody was hospitable to you. What happened? How did it feel?

A good friend noted many years ago, "Churches can learn a lot about hospitality if they pay attention to good restaurants." A thriving restaurant is always expecting new people. Strangers are warmly greeted, even directed toward a good seat. Fresh drink and warm bread are offered before the newcomers even ask. Questions are answered, no matter how apparently small or trivial. There was nothing that intentionally excluded, no insider jargon, no assigned seats, no dress code, nor inappropriate demand. It's as if they are expecting you to come, and glad when you do. That's how a restaurant does it. If the food is tasty and nutritious, there is a good chance the visitors will return.

This is more than friendliness. Most congregations regard themselves as friendly. They say, "We are a friendly church." To translate: some of us have been here forever, and we greet the others who have been here forever, and some of us who are insiders have become friends. That's a very different thing than creating space for somebody you do not know.

Hospitality originates in an open heart. That is why it is difficult – if we do not know the stranger, we might grow fearful of the stranger. But to have an open heart, to welcome someone with an open heart, is to take a significant risk: that stranger might change me! The stranger may have different view on matters that seemed settled, and that pushes me to enlarge my understanding. They could have significant needs, and that challenges me to care more deeply. They may come from a set of different life experiences, which presses me beyond my assumptions and privileges.

As Henri Nouwen writes, "If we expect any salvation, redemption, healing and new life, the first thing we need is an open receptive place where something can happen to us."[17] The change comes, not merely to the stranger, but to all of us, for all of us in some sense are strangers too. The good news of the gospel is that Jesus, who is also a stranger, comes into our midst. He comes with a challenging voice, a fierce clarity, and a grace that sounds unbelievable. His love comes with a surgical precision that can heal the hurts that we have quickly dismissed and covered over.

So, I take Father Nouwen to say if there will be salvation, redemption, healing and new life, they will come by welcoming Christ the stranger, the unexpected one, who brings us the power of God. And one of the specific ways we welcome Christ and God is by welcoming the strangers that he sends to us.

This is a challenge. Some of us remember the voices of our parents. They advised us by declaring, "Don't talk to people who don't know, don't make eye contact with them, don't allow yourself to be vulnerable in any way, for 'stranger' rhymes with 'danger.'" Making room for a stranger can feel like a threat. Many prefer to build walls, wire up security systems, and put more police on their block. They would rather live in fear than freedom. They prefer isolation to authentic human community.

Yet sometimes the stranger, like Jesus, comes anyway. My mother often warned us not to talk to outsiders. But she also liked having a full house. Four children weren't enough, so we found ourselves opening our home to exchange students. Over the years, we hosted at least seventeen different foreign students, living with us from two weeks to a full year. When I would go home during college breaks, there would be somebody different sleeping in my bedroom. I was exiled to a cot in the basement to make room for the mayor's daughter from Ecuador, the shy scientist from Tokyo, the perky blonde from Stockholm, or the industrialist's son from Berlin. When they were in our home, they were treated like sons and daughters. It was an important lesson for me to ponder on my basement cot, and in time I came to embrace it.

As I grew up and began to study the New Testament, I came to understand the profound truth at the heart of all Christian faith: that all of us are guests at God's table. None of us own the church; it is God's church. None of us can stake a claim on any of these pews; they are God's pews. Since we are guests, we are called to make room for all the other guests. We welcome them as they are, not as we prefer them to be. In the incredible mercy of God, all of us are welcomed. If we can perceive this holy hospitality, we will be cracked open, released from our self-defined isolation, and brought into the presence of others who could benefit from the same truth and grace that God has offered to us.

This lies at the very heart of the gospel. The apostle Paul said as much to a Christian congregation in Rome, a church full of people that he had never met. "Welcome one another," he said, "just as Christ as welcomed you, for the glory of God."(Romans 15:7) It's not merely good advice for a friendly bunch of Christians. This is the clear reminder that God's glory is revealed among a group of people who make room for one another. We are more than names on a stick-on name tag. Each of us is a living story, a breathing soul, hungry for the kind of love that takes us seriously.

That can happen. Among those who are spiritually alert, it does happen. At a recent gathering of folks who are interested in joining our congregation, one of the participants said she didn't know many people in our church or our town. It took a lot of courage to say that out loud, in a room of strangers. Next thing we knew, the newcomer who was sitting next to her invited her to her home that afternoon. I am certain there were some fresh-baked cookies when she arrived.

God is glorified when people make room for one another. It's called hospitality. We may think we offer this gift to somebody else, but we can only offer it because God has first offered it to us. The truth is all of us are guests at God's table. Hospitality is one of God's guests making room for another guest.

I remember the miracle of that evening on the island of Iona. There we were, my wife and I, strangers in a room of strangers. We were each invited to sit with other strangers around us. She struck up a short conversation with an engineering student from Manchester, as I met a young architect from Belgium. Then all of us worshiped together.

We sang to a God who gathers us in, prayed to a Savior who loves us all, and gave our offerings to the Spirit who nudges us beyond our tendencies to stick to ourselves.

There is gospel in such a moment. Jesus said to all his fellow strangers, "Whoever welcomes you welcomes me, and whoever welcomes me welcomes the one who sent me." Jesus flips the practice of hospitality inside out. Life and faith and church are not primarily about what *we* do, what *we* believe, and whom *we* want to welcome. Life, faith, and church are defined by who reached us, who welcomed us, and whose lives are affected because of us.

This, too, is the work of Christ, ever enlarging the circle. He invites us to offer a cold cup of water to those who thirst. This is at least as important as learning the name and life story of the person in the next pew or finding a home for an immigrant family from another country. "Whoever welcomes you welcomes me," he said. He meant it.

In fact, near the end of his time among us, Jesus told a true story about the future. He said the day would come when all truth will be revealed, and all people will be sorted. The single question at the heart of God's judgment is whether people have opened their hearts to those around them. As the risen Lord will say, "I was a stranger and you welcomed me." Everybody will be astonished, he declared, and every single person will ask, "Lord, when was it that we saw you a stranger and welcomed you?"

Remember what he said? "Truly I tell you, just as you welcome one of the least of these, members of my family, you did it to me."(Mathew 25:31-46)

This is important stuff. It is so important that, very early in Christian history, a group of monks agreed that whenever a guest came to their monastery, they would open the door and say, "Welcome, Christ!" They did not want to miss the opportunity. As Saint Benedict wrote in his rule of faith, "All guests who present themselves are to be welcomed as Christ."[18]

One time, I checked into a monastery for a few days of prayer and study. As I signed the visitors register, I heard the guest master say it out loud, "Welcome, Christ!" I looked from signing my name and said, "Better safe than sorry?"

He smiled and replied, "Better to be open-hearted than shriveled up."

Matthew 11:16-19, 25-30

Rest

I don't know of a more inviting invitation: "Come to me and I will give you rest." Jesus speaks to the woman who cannot sleep, to the child who is anxious, and to the man is bone-tired. Come ... rest. The invitation is gentle, not forceful. He speaks from a level place, a humble place. His invitation includes all: "all you," or as they say in the South, "y'all." There's not a single person excluded. Everybody come, come and rest.

What intrigues me is why so many people turn him down. Have you ever noticed that?

As a kid, I learned from my father how to put in a long day's work. At his desk by eight every morning, home for supper by six, then he would change his clothes and go outside for a few more hours of labor. Dad came from a family of farmers. They didn't sit very much, unless Grandpa was riding the red tractor in his straw hat and a strand of timothy grass in his teeth. Even then, the days were long and there was precious little rest.

When we would visit those grandparents, we'd leave at the end of a workday. Mom would have the kids bundled up and ready go. Dad would roar up the street, run in and change his clothes, and off we'd go, six hours in the car, along the endless road. Next morning, he would wake early on his parents' farm, slug down some coffee, and ask if there was anything he could do to help. He didn't rest when he went on vacation.

There are a lot of people like that. They can quote the Bible: *"Idle hands are the devil's workshop,"*(Proverbs 16:27, TLB) says one version of a verse from the book of Proverbs. (Proverbs 16:27) Or there is that section that somebody read to us at dawn at the teenage Bible camp:

> *Go to the ant, O sluggard; consider her ways, and be wise. Without having any chief, officer, or ruler, she prepares her food in summer, and gathers her sustenance in harvest. How long will you lie there, O sluggard? When will you arise from your sleep? A little sleep, a little slumber, a little folding of the hands to rest, and poverty will come upon you like a vagabond, and want like an armed man.*(Proverbs 6: 6 – 11 RSV)

This is a compelling lesson from nature. In case you don't know what a "sluggard" is, the New Revised Standard translates the word as "lazybones." Go the hard working ant, O lazybones, and learn your lesson. Work hard. Don't ever sit still. The Calvinists didn't invent a hard work ethic. They found it in their Bibles.

But there is also the invitation to rest. According to the Greek dictionary, to rest is "to cease from movement or labor in order to recover and collect (one's) strength." Now, we don't need a dictionary to tell us that. We already know what rest is. But we don't do it very well.

As Jesus suggested, this is a matter of the soul. "Come to me," he said, "and I will give you rest for your souls." The soul is the part of us that's alive. It's the intersection of thought, feeling, and breath. It is the gift breathed into us by God's Spirit that makes us human. The soul is the wellspring of our dreams, the anchor for our imagination, the seat of all passion and hope.

The soul is the part of us that can be traumatized, anxious, and fearful. When the soul is wounded, one of the typical responses is to keep pushing on, persisting through, often in the vain hope that if we just add another inch to the span of our day, we will speed by or gloss over the deep wound that we are trying to avoid.

That's what Wayne Muller identified as he reflected the practice of keeping sabbath – and why so many people resist it. He wrote:

> This is one of our fears of quiet; if we stop and listen, we will hear this emptiness. If we worry we are not good or whole inside, we will be reluctant to stop and rest, afraid we will find a lurking emptiness, a terrible, aching void with nothing to fill it, as if it will corrode and destroy us like some horrible, insatiable monster. If we are terrified of what we will find in rest, we will refuse to look up from our work, refuse to stop moving. We quickly fill all the blanks on our calendar with tasks, accomplishments, errands, things to be done ... anything to fill the time, the empty space.[19]

He is right about that. Go to a restaurant and watch the people around you. Some of them would rather stay attached to their smart phones than have an intelligent conversation. Go the shore to get away from it all, and when you realize that others had the same idea, take note of how many of them are staying tethered to email and internet.

It is simply the next extension of what I discovered about two weeks after I bought my first laptop computer some 25 years ago: because we can do work anywhere, we never stop working, especially if the work is mental, emotional, virtual, or expected of us.

Let me tell you it was demanding to spend some recent time in a desert where there was little internet service, and cell phone service was available if you stood on a table with your left arm in the air as an antenna. Don't ask how I discovered about the cell phone service.

So what is the rest that restores our souls? That is the invitation of Jesus Christ. We find it by "coming to him." *And what is that?* Coming to a church? No, we come to him. If you merely come to church, it will exhaust you.

But we can't see him. How do we come to him? I think we come by paying attention to his grace. We come by listening to Jesus say that every one of us has inestimable value. We come by chewing on his promise that we "do not live by bread alone," but by the life-giving words that come from the mouth of God. We come by observing the birds of the air and how they are cared for by an unseen benevolence. We come by admiring the wildflowers which bring beauty to life's path and we did not plant them.

Life is all about grace, the invisible goodness and favor which give us our lives in the first place. If we're convinced that life is only weariness and burden, then we're missing how everything is really a gift, a generous gift. If we are obsessed with the latest stupid stunt of some public figure, then we're missing what a wonderful blessing it is to be together, to pursue the dreams we have in common, to work for the benefit of all of us.

Maybe the saddest addiction of all is to be consumed only with myself – my views, my fears, my worries, my hurts, my anger, my wounds. I don't know if there is a heavier burden than that. There is only one way to have that burden lifted from our shoulders. It is to come to Christ, who alone is saving the world as an expression of the goodness and grace of God. We really do have to give up the burden of being addicted to ourselves.

I recently picked up the latest collection of sabbath poems by Wendell Berry, the Kentucky farmer. For forty years, he has spent Sundays resting, going for a walk, and writing short poems on sabbath themes. He pays attention to the world that thrives even on his sabbath day off. In the book's preface he wrote these words:

We are to rest on the sabbath in order
to understand that the providence or the
productivity of the living world, the most essential
work, continues while we rest. This work is
entirely independent of our work, and is far more
complex and wonderful than any work we have
ever done or will ever do. It is more complex and
beautiful than we will ever understand.[20]

The world doesn't revolve around us. It would be better for us to orbit around the one who made it all, the one who fills it with life and brings it to such abundance.

"Come to me ... and I will give you rest." That's why the invitation persists. We don't rest once and then think we're done with it. Neither do we sit on our hands while others labor to benefit us. A full life is a rhythm of work and rest, of task and reflection. And if life is out of balance, if the rhythm is limping, the invitation is to come, to keep coming, to persist in coming to the grace of Jesus Christ.

At its heart, this kind of rest is about one thing: what will fill me with God's abundant life? What will restore my soul? What are the practices that create a song in my heart? What is it, for you, that brings you totally alive? That's the kind of rest we're talking about.

Every one of us has an answer uniquely based on who they are, how they are growing, and how they are wondrously made. In my house, my wife picks up yarn and needles, and imagines a hat for a premature infant; although these days, she is just as likely to design and create a kitchen table or a backyard deck. It is an awesome thing to be married to a woman with a nail gun. Meanwhile I sit in my blue chair, juggling metaphors or scratching out a new jazz melody. All of us are wired differently.

The lady up the street has an enormous flower garden; tending it is what gives her life. Or there's the man who persists in welcoming cast-off puppies; they keep him company and he returns the favor.

For some people, it's running marathons (which I can't understand) or singing difficult songs (which I do). For other people, it is providing a happy table, where joy is the main course.

For some people, it's the solitary work of quiet prayer for the needs of the world. For others, it's translating those prayers into acts of mercy and justice. It gives life to them and to others.

This is what it means to come to Christ in restorative rest. In the grace of God, we find what gives us life and we pursue it. And we keep pursuing it, not for the sake of indulgence, but in the pursuit of a greater integration and health. This is a different kind of yoke to be placed upon our shoulders. We give up all the other slaveries and take on the disciplines that heal our souls.

That's why we keep coming into this place for worship. For this is where we hear once again how much we are loved, how deeply we are saved, and how greatly the world is kept in hands far more gracious and just than our own.

May you have a blessed sabbath, again and again.

Seeds

I am always astonished at the tenacity of vegetation. The dandelion pops up overnight, blossoms in a burst of yellow, then explodes in a puff and scatters across the yard. There's a vine that wraps itself around the back fence. Every year it gets snipped down to the soil, but every year it returns and grows taller. It's well planted. Or there's the blade of grass that pokes its head out of the crack in the driveway – how did the seed get there?

A good seed, given the right conditions, can grow just about anywhere. A few years ago, my mother gave us some a few spearmint plants for the front garden. They took over. Now there's no room for anything else. The few daisies that our friend Carol shared were planted in rocky soil and they are doing just fine. While I sipped my morning coffee, I saw them greeting the morning sun and singing alleluia.

A good seed can grow just about anywhere – but not everywhere. The rocky mountain has a bald spot somewhere around ten thousand feet. The grass grows in the crack of my driveway, but not on the driveway itself. And in the summer, the sun might eventually burn out the well-lit lawn.

Jesus tosses this familiar parable toward the ears of his hearers, uncertain where it will land. There is no telling which response will happen this time.

Some of us will race ahead a paragraph or two, and find a freeze-dried, just-add-water explanation of the parable. It's given in the same style as Saint Augustine, who taught that the parables can function like a hidden code. He liked to say that every detail of the parable stood for something else. The word of God's kingdom equals the seed. Each patch of soil equals the individual listener. Rocky soil is the person with no depth. The scorching sun equals the troubles of this life. The thorns that choke out the seed are cares of the world and the lure of wealth, and so on.

This is how the early church understood the parable. It is an obvious interpretation that comes by observation. Just watch who shows up on a Sunday, and the following Sunday. Take note of who is flourishing. The gospel seed is thrown into all kinds of soil.

There are people who stumble into a church, sit down and listen, and quickly discover a life-giving word from God. They are excited. They return early the next week. They sit down front. But should they lose a job, have trouble at home, get snubbed at coffee hour, or discover that all the Christians have flaws, they may slip away. And if they hear something challenging in a sermon or a Bible study, they evaporate. Nothing grows. They are only around for the excitement, not the growth. It's easy to call that shallow soil.

Or consider the people who move into town, buy the big house, have 2.3 perfect children, and drive the big car. They come to First Presbyterian Church, because it would never occur to them to go to Last Presbyterian Church. The music is stunning, the building is well-kept, the preacher went to an important seminary, and most of the people look just like them.

But then, some friends at the club mention some wonderful vacation spots. The kids get involved in weekend sports, not because they're great athletes, but there's where their friends are. Time passes, and one of the deacons sees them in the grocery store on a Tuesday night. "It's been forever since we've been in church," they confess. "Our weekends are just so busy." The Bible says, "Cares of the world, the lure of wealth, it yields nothing."

It's easy to evaluate by the results. That may have been how John Calvin developed his views on predestination. Calvin was preaching the gospel twice a day, every day. He noticed that some people got it and others fell asleep. Some people grew in the faith while others daydreamed. Calvin said, "Obviously God has turned on the lights for some and kept the lights off for others." It never occurred to him to evaluate the quality of his sermons, but, well, he was noticing the results.

American church people love to look at the results. Where is the growth happening? Where is there a thirty-fold, sixty-fold, or hundred-fold return? Where are the other churches growing? What are they doing? What fresh ideas can we steal from them? After all, some churches will steal another church's members, tempting the second church to up their game and steal some back.

It is a distraction to look only at the results. If you look at the results, you never ask what kind of soil you are. Is this acidic soil? Are there some rocks here? Has it been paved over?

And here are a couple of even tougher questions. Have I allowed the crows to snatch the seed away from me? Are there thorns of privilege and affluence wrapping themselves around my legs?

It is a hundred times easier to look out there than it is to reflect in the mirror and ask, "Why isn't the seed of God's kingdom growing and flourishing in me?" It is a worthy question – but I don't think it has a lot to do with the parable.

This is the parable of the sower. The sower went out to sow. What did he do? He threw the seed all over the place. He showed no caution, no preparation, no hesitation, and so the seed went everywhere. He did not prepare the ground, pull up the weeds, or remove the stones. He didn't chase away the birds, block the sun, or chop down the thorns. No, he was not the gardener. He was the sower.

So let's pay attention to what we learn about him. I have made a list.

First item on the list: he had a lot of seed. He never ran out of seed. You might say he was the source of all the seed. He never had a shortage when it came to sowing the seed.

Second item on the list: this sower was terrifically generous. He threw the seed all over the place. It was not restricted to carefully dug furrows. The seed was thrown everywhere. It didn't matter if the soil was rough or welcoming. There was always fertile seed which carried its own promise within its own shell.

Third item on the list: the sower was not interested in controlling the outcome. All he wanted to do was spread the seed around as far as he could. There are all kinds of soil; for all we know, the sower may have created all that soil too. But for now, it was the season for seeding, and he was doing a marvelous job. The seed was all over.

Fourth, and maybe the most important item on the list: the sower knew if that seed was going to grow, it was going to grow. It was good quality seed, the best seed possible. In fact, it might have been the only seed there was. Its source was in the sower. It was his seed, and his seed alone.

As I reflect on this, I remembered a prophetic poem of Isaiah. Let me remind us of the pithy parts:

> *For as the rain and the snow come down from heaven, and do not return there until they have watered the earth, making it bring forth and sprout, giving seed to the sower and bread to the eater, so shall my word be that goes out from my mouth; it shall not return to me empty, but it shall accomplish that which I purpose, and succeed in the thing for which I sent it.* (Isaiah 55:10-11)

Do you know what I hear in those words? I hear that God is responsible for God's own kingdom. God gives life to the soil and the soul. God's own word will take root and flourish. That God is not concerned with wasting words but creating bread, specifically the bread of life.

Our job is not to be selective, restrictive, or evaluative. No, in the name of the sower, we are called to be generous. Keep spreading the seed of God's kingdom.

I recall a conversation with a youth group leader. She was feeling worn out. Plans would be made for the youth of our community, and few of the kids would show up. She would say, "I don't know what to do." I responded, "Keep going. You never know when the seed might take root." So she would try again. There would be little, if no response.

One day, she was getting ready to send out some information and she had two sets of labels. I said, "Why two sets of labels?" Well, one was the A List, and the other was the B List. The A List comprised the few kids who were a sure bet to come – they loved the program, or their parents forced them to come, or maybe both. The B List named the kids who never came. The information was only going to get sent to the A List. She said, "Why should we waste the invitation on the ones who never come?"

I simply said, "Because you never know." You never really know. This is not harvest time yet. It's sowing time. And God has a way of creating life where you can't imagine it possible. Come over and look at the grass sprouting up in the cracks of my driveway.

Now if you have ears to hear, and you hear this parable of Jesus, and if you flinch when you hear him speak of "shallow soil" or "the thorns that choke out the seed, due to the cares of the world or the lure of wealth," pay attention to that. Make the necessary changes that you might welcome "the life that really is life."(1 Timothy 6:19)

Every week, I meet people on the street or in the stores, and they say, "Oh, I don't get to church as much as I should." Or "it's been a while since I've been to church." Or "Hey stranger, I bet you've been missing me." Well, of course I've been missing you. It's good for us to be together, if only for an hour a week.

But we cannot change anybody's schedule for them. I am powerless to rearrange anybody else's priorities. It is not my role to cancel somebody's trip to the shore or declare that travel soccer is the bane of all Christian educators. It's up to each of us to consider what we might do to welcome the word that God speaks, to nourish it in our hearts, and take part in the fruitfulness of the gospel of God.

Let's keep our eyes on the sower. As for me, I want to sow the seed of the kingdom, as God sows the seed: generously, lovingly, without restriction, because I have seen what happens when the love of God takes root in a person's life. The hopeless brighten like summer daisies. The drunkard sells his beer and buys furniture. The self-centered suburbanite befriends the poor. The old crank transforms into Santa Claus. The fractured souls are healed.

The gospel bears abundant fruit. It is just as the sower intended.

Matthew 13:24-30, 36-43

Weeds

One summer day, it was my turn to mow the yard. The dew had burned off, the grass was dry. I fired up the Briggs and Stratton, lowered the blade, and took it for a spin. The job took about 45 minutes and it was done.

Yet as I circled the front yard for the first time, I realized my lawn is full of weeds. Now I knew there were a few. A weed-and-feed expedition earlier in the spring eliminated most of the dandelions. It seems other undesirables have invaded our plot of land.

That is a big deal in the town where I live. Everybody wants a perfect yard. A perfect yard represents a perfect home. Some neighbors spend a lot of money to have professional chemists spray their soil. Most of these consumers want a guarantee that they will remain weed-free, even though such a guarantee is not worth the paper it is written on.

One man tried a number of lawn services, to no avail. Being a tightly controlled sort, the weeds greatly upset him. One year, in a scorched earth attempt, he killed all the vegetation on his property. He wiped it all out, grass included. Then he trucked in a lot of top soil and spread it around. With the best Scotts Premium tall fescue he could buy, he reseeded the entire yard. Guess what? The grass came up. It was beautiful. The weeds came back. They had to send him to a padded room for a short vacation.

Where do the weeds come from? This is the recurring question in lawn care and life. If Jesus says, "the kingdom of heaven is like a gardener who throws around a lot of seed," his very next episode is about the reality of weeds.

There are weeds in every family: even if the kids are raised with safety and good nutrition and the grandparents are healthy, somebody gets sick, somebody else goes off the rails, and somehow there is always a crazy uncle. It would be nice to think every family is perfect, but we know better. There are weeds.

There are weeds in every business. The enterprise is created, the product identified, the factory built, the workers are trained. And then a machine breaks down, or one of the workers sneaks out a product under his shirt, or somebody in the financial department is caught cooking the books. Weeds!

There are weeds in every church. We don't want to believe that, but it is true. Good people respond to the casting about of the seed of the gospel. They congregate, they sing, they worship, they declare their love for Jesus and one another. Suddenly a bit of gossip invades like a pestilence. Or a weak soul is tempted by all that goodness. Or something sinister happens in the dark shadows of the choir room. Weeds!

It is difficult to deal with the reality of weeds. When a young adult went looking for his first house, he found a possible home in a nearby village, took a tour, and came back laughing. "I crossed it off the list immediately," he said. "The owner had paved over the front yard." That's one response to the weeds, I suppose.

Or there is that middle-aged minister that I know. They said he was "seasoned;" I think they mean "worn out." He said he was going to start a new church. There would be a steeple, a sanctuary, and one pew large enough for only one person: him. "That's the kind of church I want," he said. "Just me and God, nobody else." No weeds in the garden.

In the parable that we've heard, the servants come to the owner of the house and ask, "Should we pull up the weeds?" It's a reasonable question. The landowner is the sower who has cast about "the good seed." It was pure and perfect as he threw it about. But then something happened. Some kind of corruption crept in.

It is easy to ascribe that to an enemy, to some unseen villain who sneaks in late at night and taints a perfect crop. Now, I know – that's ridiculous in real life. My next door neighbor throws broken tree branches back into my yard, but I don't believe she would ever sneak over and blow dandelion seeds in our direction. Well, she might – but I don't perceive her as "an enemy."

I wonder if the landowner is overstating the case. There are some weak-hearted Christians who think the devil is as powerful as God, but that's nonsense. God made the world. God made the squirrels and the pine cones and the sea turtles and the silver mountains. Then God called it all of it "good." There's no devil with that kind of power. The devil is a liar; he's never as important as he says he is.

But there is corruption. God's good creation is mysteriously tainted. The psalmist knew that; for instance, Psalm 12 with its final verse: "On every side the wicked prowl, as vileness is exalted among humankind." Maybe you came to church to forget about that, but church is about reality. The reality is there are some weeds in the wheat. The parable says, "When the wheat bears its grain, that's when the weeds become obvious."

The question is what do we do about that? If there is good and there is evil, some want to pluck out the evil. Pull the weeds. That is an understandable response.

Every once in a while, you hear about somebody who wants to purify the world, or at least their corner of it. They will go in there and separate the weeds from the wheat, the tainted from the pure, the evil from the good, the goats from the sheep, the left from the right. They are on a crusade to restore things to the way they were intended to be. We might even hear somebody come along and say, "I'm going to drain the swamp."

Well, how do you think that is going to work it? It will not work so well if the swamp is already inside of you. It is impossible to clean up the world if your own hands are dirty. And do you know why that is? Because the enticements of corruption are always greater than the purity of those who think they are good.

And once in a while someone will try to start pulling the weeds. A church leader may look around, see some empty seats, and say, "We are carrying some people on the membership list who do not come, do not participate, or do not give. It's time to clear the roll." This is usually said with the best of intentions. But if there's a problem with the initiative, it's the presumption that "I alone" – or "we alone" – can call ourselves pure, and point to "they" who are not. With all pastoral authority, I say get off it.

Every so often in my pastoral work, I come across a dear soul who wishes to divide the world into two categories: "Christian" and "Everybody else." And they are absolutely convinced that they know what "Christian" means. There is usually a checklist of a lot of observable behaviors, like "don't drink, don't dance, don't chew, or date the girls that do." Why do we have to reduce the Christian faith to observable behaviors? Should we ever make decisions based on mercy? Forgiveness? Love? A second chance?

Perhaps the dear soul might say, "We shouldn't put that person on a committee because he's not Christian." Or "She's not Christian enough." You know what that is? It's a desire to pull the weeds, to keep the field pure, to present the church to Christ spotless and without blemish.

It sounds so right but it can go so wrong, because all of us are a work in progress. It is not harvest time yet. And who made any of us the arbiter of who is Christian and who is not? Who gets to decide who belongs to God and who does not? Who has enough purity to weed the garden?

According to the New Testament, it is Jesus Christ alone who will present the church spotless and without blemish. And do you know how he can do it? Because he has forgiven every sin.(Ephesians 5:25-27) So Jesus is the one who says, "Leave the weeds alone. Don't touch them. Don't uproot the good wheat by presuming you can identify and extract a weed."

One of the intriguing details of this parable is that the "weeds" actually have a proper name. In Greek, they are called "*zizania*" What's *zizania*? It is a plant that looks just like wheat, probably what contemporary botanists call "darnel." The point is when *zizania* grows alongside wheat, you can't tell the difference. You cannot distinguish. You cannot differentiate.

So the parable suggests what Jesus has said before: "Do not judge, lest you be judged." Our own vision is not clear. Our own clarity is more obscured than we realize. And maybe there are a few weeds in our own garden. God still has to do some work in us.

John Calvin, the ancient reformer, learned this lesson from Jesus. For all his clarity and righteousness, Calvin would never finally conclude that he himself was righteous or clear. He would say that everybody, no matter how pure they believe themselves to be, that everybody bears the seed of corruption. Even our best efforts can be tainted by self-interest and twisted out of shape by evil.

So if you think you might be pulling up the weeds, you could end up destroying the wheat, the good crop of wheat. This is why we need a Savior, somebody who sees clearly and ultimately will do the final sorting. The day will come, said Christ, when the fisherman's net has caught all kinds of fish, and the good will be separated from the bad. (Matthew 13:47-50) The day will come, he said, when the sheep will be separated from the goats, all on the basis of whether or not they learned to show compassion and care. (Matthew 25:31-46)

Jesus said, "Leave it alone." When it's harvest time, better hands than ours will handle it. In the meantime Jesus never said we should acquiesce to "the evils that we deplore." Faithful Christian discipleship always works for good. It works for God's good, and it works for the public good. We must never be naïve and declare "everything is beautiful." Neither must we give in to the evil and say with cynicism, "There's nothing we can do."

A number of years ago, columnist David Brooks interviewed a young politician named Barack Obama. It was a genial conversation, and Brooks discerned that Mr. Obama read a lot of books. Suddenly Brooks asked out of the blue, "Have you ever read the theologian Reinhold Niebuhr?"

Obama sat up straight and said, "I love him. He's one of my favorite philosophers." Brooks said, "What do you take away from him?"

With a rush of words, Obama said, "I take away the compelling idea that there's serious evil in the world, and hardship and pain. We should be humble and modest in our belief we can eliminate those things. But we shouldn't use that as an excuse for cynicism and inaction. I take away the sense we have to make these efforts knowing they are hard. We cannot swing from naïve idealism to bitter realism."[21]

I was thinking about all of this while I was mowing my heavily weed-filled lawn. It gave me a lot to think about. It was a hot day, so when I was finished, I asked the Lord if he wanted to join me for a cup of cold water. We sat down on my front porch and had a little chat.

He looked at the front yard and said, "It looks pretty good. Your wife will be proud of you." I said, "Thanks, Lord. It's a job that needed to get done."

We sat for a minute. I took a sip of that delicious cup of water. Then I got up the courage to ask, "But what about the weeds? There are so many weeds. Even if I had the energy or the inclination, I could never get rid of the weeds."

He smiled and said, "Leave it alone."
I started to say, "But the weeds…"
He interrupted me to say, "It's my field."[22]

Catholic

It never fails. Say it's a Sunday morning when we have a baptism. There is a mixed crowd of long-timers and newcomers. The baby is beautiful, the family is all smiles, the Presbyterians are delighted. And then at the door, one of the newcomers says, "Why in the world did you say, 'We believe in the catholic church?'"

She is referring to the Apostles' Creed , of course, and curious why we would say such a thing. With a smile, I usually respond that nobody has a proprietary lock on the word "catholic." There is Roman Catholic and Polish National Catholic, and people in both camps have assured me that they have little to do with one another. I once heard a Russian Orthodox priest tell me that nobody is catholic – much less orthodox – except for the likes of him and those who agree with him. I answered, "Really? I thought those evaluations were above our pay grade."

"I believe in the one holy catholic church." We say that a lot around here, almost every week, but I'm guessing that we really don't give it much thought. We say "catholic" with a small "c." We tell the inquisitors that means "universal," as in "the big church, the complete church, the everywhere church,' the "one in the Spirit, one in the Lord" church.

Perhaps they've been shaped to still fight the Reformation, as some of us were instructed long ago to keep the battles blazing. If you talk to some of our denomination who live in a town with a strong ethnic identity and ask, "What makes you Presbyterian?" they might very well reply, "We're not Cat'lic." Except that Jesus says, "Maybe they are."

What does it mean to be the catholic church? Or better stated, the church catholic?

All of this arose for me when I heard again the second parable from today's text. "The kingdom of heaven is like yeast. A woman mixes it into some flour until *the whole thing* is leavened."

On first reading, it is the phase "the whole thing" that catches the ear. *Holos* is the Greek word for "the whole thing," the same *holos* that is smack dab in the middle of the word "catholic." Catholic is "the whole thing," not just one small part of it, but the whole thing.

That pushes a bigger question – is the Christian church, or one slice of it, the sum of all God's activity in the world? To sharpen the question and provide a good answer, we have the words of Frederick Buechner, the Presbyterian writer and wit. He says there is a visible church, and an invisible church. The people who show up on a Sunday morning constitute the visible, he notes. Their names are written in a membership directory, listed as ushers or choir members, and they are present for any observer to see.

The invisible church consists of the people who do the will of God in the world. Not always visible, nor known to the regular pew sitters, God knows who they are and utilizes them to further the mission of heaven.

With this, Buechner quipped, "Think of them as two circles. The optimist says they are concentric. The cynic says they don't even touch. The realist says they occasionally overlap."[23]

His point was simply that God is at work in the whole world, not merely in the church. And sometimes the church does God's will ... and always the church's prayer is answered, "Thy will be done." In other words, "catholic" refers to the "whole thing," to *all* of God's activity.

Needless to say, that's a lot more activity that we can comprehend, which is precisely the one detail in Jesus' parable. How much flour are we talking about? "Three measures." Biblically speaking, how much is that? That's about a bushel of flour, about 128 cups. That's sixteen five-pound bags. And when you add in the forty-two cups of water to make it come together, you have about a hundred pounds of dough. That's an enormous amount of flour, enough to bake enough bread to feed a large crowd of people.

This woman in the parable, this kingdom woman, is working in the yeast in all of that flour. Imagine that!

If you can picture it in your head, you know her work is going to take a while. This is not a rush job, and neither is the work of God. Maybe you have noticed God is in no particular hurry. We pray, we trust that somebody is listening, we trust our prayers will receive some kind of answer. But if your prayers are anything like my prayers, the most frequent answer is "Wait and see."

This woman is working an enormous pile of dough, and she is working the *whole thing*.

The second thing we know, especially if we've ever worked with yeast, is that the whole thing is going to rise. Yeast works in secret. You work it in, you leave it alone, and it does its thing. Amy Jill Levine, the Bible scholar, pointed out that Jesus referred to a certain kind of yeast. It's a sourdough starter. It ferments the flour. The whole thing bubbles up if you just give it some time.

That's the promise of God's dominion, what Christ calls "the kingdom." It bubbles up, it grows. It rises in secret and the whole thing is a mystery.

Consider the history of Christianity in China. In 1949, Mao Tse-tung came to power and threw out all the Christian missionaries. He set up a secular state and outlawed any Christian activity. During the Cultural Revolution, all religious life was officially banned in China. After Mao's death and the partial opening up of China, somebody discovered there were over 67 million Christians now in the country – and our missionaries weren't over there doing the converting. This is a glimpse of how God's kingdom will rise.

The whole thing is a mystery. Like that little mustard seed, so small, so inconsequential, so inadequate, such an unlikely metaphor in that previous parable Jesus offers. Yet the little mustard seed grows into an enormous bush, so large that the sparrows come and make their nests there. How does something so small grow to be so large? How does sourdough yeast ferment in secret and enlarge an enormous lump of dough?

The biologists will remind us that yeast itself is a living organism, a single cell living organism. Quite literally, when someone massages in the sourdough starter yeast, they are infusing that lump of flour with life. So it's no wonder that Jesus invites us to look within the mysteries from the field and the kitchen, and wonder at the quiet, mysterious, life-giving work of God.

It is important to keep this clear. Often, we Americans latch onto stories of explosive growth and enormous size, as if bigger is always better. Have you ever heard those tales? The little corner grocery becomes a massive chain of stores. The guy who built gadgets in the garage creates a worldwide technology business. The living room Bible study becomes a megachurch, and so on. None of these scenarios equate to the kingdom of heaven, mostly because they are about us and our own efforts.

By contrast, remember what Jesus said about the kingdom. It's all upside down:

- What is greatness in the kingdom of heaven? To become like a small, trusting child. (Matthew 18:4)
- Who is first in the kingdom of heaven? The last. (Matthew 19:30)
- Who receives the blessings of the kingdom of heaven? The poor in spirit, the meek, the peacemakers, and those thirsty for justice. (Matthew 5:3-9)

In God's kingdom, there is no room for any kind of arrogance, self-promotion, or violence, because it is God's kingdom. It is God who rules over the kingdom of heaven. And that kingdom is not located on a distant cloud sometime in the afterlife. Rather, it is the very quality of life for which Jesus teaches us to pray: the will of God, on earth as it already is in heaven (Matthew 6:10). This is what grows. This is what rises. Not the accomplishment or the arrogance of humanity, but the rule of God over all life.

The apostle Paul could testify to this. He wrote a letter to a church in Rome, full of people he had never met. And he declared on the largest possible screen, "All things work together for God for those who love God." It was meant to be. God's will is predestined. The kingdom is going to happen.

It grows with us or without us. The good seed sprouts up in receptive soil. The good crop lasts among the weeds. Like an otherwise insignificant mustard seed, it digs deep roots and extends wide and hospitable branches. And all of this happens because of God. God makes it grow. Or to put it another way, wherever there is growth in love, mercy, and justice, God is there, extending his rule until the final day it is everywhere.

So the word for today is "catholic," as in "the whole thing." As in the huge lump of dough where God is already in the kitchen, working in the yeast until it becomes inseparable from the flour.

I don't know, really, what all of this means. I certainly don't have a cute little story to bring it home. All we have is a one sentence parable. It is a little bitty parable, as small as its own mustard seed, and it offers a glimpse of a truth much larger than our heads and hearts can comprehend.

For here is that truth, as far as I know it: we are part of something so much greater than we can understand. Call it "the salvation of the world," or "the redemption of the universe," or "the invitation to come home to the Garden of Eden." Call it whatever you can, even though none of our words will ever contain it completely.

Jesus calls it the "kingdom of heaven." It comes in the assurance that nothing will ever separate us from the love of God. God's love is already planted like a little bit of yeast in a great big lump of dough. Just wait – everything will rise.

The lady at the back door said, "Why do you say the word 'catholic'? It's not your word."

I smiled and said, "It's not your word, either. It's God's word."

Trust me when I tell you that, just like a lump of yeast-filled dough, everything that belongs to God will rise.

If There Isn't Enough To Go Around

Nobody could blame the disciples for their concern. It had been a long and exhausting day. People from all over the countryside had followed Jesus with their aches and pains. Rather than retreat or rest, the gospel of Matthew tells us that Jesus sat there and saved all of them, one at a time.

Meanwhile his twelve followers were overwhelmed by the need. It was getting late, and all they could see was a long line of needy people who would not go away. "Lord," they said, "there isn't enough food to go around. Send these people away so they can get something to eat."

Here is a story we can understand. The needs of the world are overwhelming. What can we do? Where would we start? Our resources are so limited and the needs are so great. A third of the world's people are starving for food. Many more are hungry for something more.

A man named Kevin recently returned from a trip to Ethiopia. His church is building a relationship with a congregation in Ethiopia, and he went to the country to meet people in the church. He returned shocked by the hunger in Addis Ababa. In the capital city, there is a sea of humanity begging for money or food. Most beggars are little children. The guide said, "Stay away from them and watch out for pickpockets."

At one point, someone bumped into Kevin and stuck a hand in his pocket. Kevin grabbed the person's wrist and started yelling at him. The man screamed back. They did not understand one another. Kevin let him go. A few minutes later, Kevin realized he was missing some coins from his other pocket. The total value was about two American dollars, but it made him angry. He caught up with his fellow travelers, his hands now guarding his pockets.

Meanwhile one hand after another reached out for help. "Money, mister? Mister, some money? Money please?"

After a few blocks of that, Kevin's anger had subsided. What are a couple of bucks when so many people have so little? Kevin said, "I could be a millionaire and give everything away to those people, and it would not make a dent in their situation."

What do you do? The need is so great. The resources are so few. There wasn't enough to go around. Do you know how that feels?

Your church knows how it feels. Every November, the leaders of this congregation sharpen their pencils and work on the budget. We want to glorify God by providing a full range of programs, reaching out to the needy, and meeting some established obligations. And when we meet to prepare the next year's budget, there's always a shadow of disappointment that falls over the group. We never seem to have enough money to do the things that God calls us to do.

The needs are great. It seems like we have so little. We can understand this story about a multitude of hungry people who are approached with a couple of fish and five loaves of bread. The resources never seem to stretch far enough. Nobody is surprised to hear the disciples say, "Lord, send them away."

According to the gospel of Matthew, however, Jesus did not let his fishermen off the hook. As surely as this story of feeding the multitude is about Jesus, the founder of the feast, it is also a story about his twelve disciples. When the twelve said, "Lord, get rid of this crowd," he replied, "*You* give them something to eat!" Now that's a striking aspect to this story. Jesus did not turn stones into loaves of bread to feed the crowd. Instead he demanded his followers to pitch in and give what they had. The gospel of Matthew insists the disciples gave their own bread and fish. There is no mention of a young boy who offered his lunch; that's the gospel of John. This is Matthew, and in Matthew, Jesus said, "*You* give them something to eat."

They responded, "All we have are five loaves and a couple of fish." So he asked for it. They gave Jesus everything they possessed. He thanked God for it. He broke the bread. And he gave them back the bread in order for them to give it away to others. After the crowds ate their fill, they took up the leftovers.

By the way: did you hear how many baskets were left over? There were twelve baskets of bread left! That's one for each disciple. Isn't that something? They gave everything to Jesus. He blessed it, broke it, gave it back to be given away. In the economy of God, the disciples who gave everything to the Lord received everything they needed in return.

Do you suppose God still works like that? We hope so. We would like to think we could give everything to God and get all we need in return. Unfortunately such a great economy breaks down somehow. Our hearts may be convicted by the great needs of the church or the world, but we grow afraid. The fists clench shut. The purse closes. The wallet snaps shut. It takes a direct intervention to change us.

It reminds me of the preacher who was leading the people in worship one day. It was time for the weekly offering and she said, "I want all of you to stand up for a minute." Everybody stood. Then she said, "I want all of you to lean forward, grab the wallet or purse of the person in front of you, and give as you always wanted to, but never had the chance." That would be fun, wouldn't it? And giving ought to be fun!

But the opposite of generosity is fear. We look at what little we have, and we think of the reasons why we cannot help. D.H. Lawrence told a story about a family with a boy and two little girls. They lived in a nice house with a garden. Yet the family felt an anxiety: there was never enough money. Both mother and father had small incomes, but they didn't have enough to reach the social position they desired. The father pursued business leads that never materialized. The mother tried to earn more money, but her failures etched deep lines into her face.

In time, their home became haunted with the unspoken phrase, "There must be more money." No one ever said it aloud, least of all the children. But the words filled the home, especially when expensive toys filled the nursery.

> Behind the shining modern rocking-horse,
> behind the smart doll's house, a voice would
> start whispering: "There must be more money.
> There must be more money." The children could
> hear it all the time, though nobody said it aloud.

And the children would stop playing, to listen,
for a moment. They would look into each other's
eyes, to see if they had all heard. And each one
saw in the eyes of the other two that they too had
heard. "There must be more money. There must
be more money." Yet nobody ever said it aloud.
The whisper was everywhere, and therefore
no one spoke it. Just as no one ever says, "We
are breathing," in spite of the fact that breath is
coming and going all the time.[24]

Did you ever hear that haunting whisper in your
home? I'm talking about that quiet voice says, "There
must be more money." Meanwhile, money keeps coming
and going all the time.

Jesus intervened by saying, "*You* give them something
to eat. *You* teach your neighbors how to pray. *You* send
out missionaries to address the world's aches and pains.
You sing the hymns that praise God's name. *You* give your
money to further the work of the church."

Usually our first response is to look down and say,
"We don't have what it takes," or "We don't have the
ability," or "We don't have the money." Then to ease our
consciences, we drive off to the Mammon Warehouse and
buy a few things we don't need.

It strikes me that Jesus took whatever his disciples
gave him, in this case, two fish and five loaves. After he
thanked God, he broke what they had given him, and
said, "Now, give it away." He broke their gifts of bread.
They could no longer hold them, hoard them, keep them,
preserve them, or protect them. Instead they were broken,
so that everybody could have a piece.

Oh, if we could only dare to let that happen! We're so afraid there isn't going to be enough food or money or whatever else to go around. So we start stockpiling it. Or we use more than our share. You've heard statistics like that. The United States has only 5.6% of the world's population. Yet we consume 42% of the world's aluminum, 33% of the world's copper, 44% of the world's coal, 33% of the world's petroleum, and 63% of the world's natural gases.[25]

Why do we do it? Is it because we are afraid there isn't going to be enough to go around? Oh, if God would only give us new eyes, that we could see our circumstances in relation to the needs of the world! Oh, if God would only give us new hearts, so we could trust God to take our offerings and do something beautiful with them! Oh, if God would only take our prized possessions and break them into something new, so that the hungry would be fed and the good news would be proclaimed!

The more I think about it, the more I realize stewardship is a matter of conversion. Those of us in the western world live with the myth of scarcity, even though the world is filled with signs of God's abundant generosity. We need to be converted, so we might become generous just like God. That is especially true for those of us who have so much, yet are convinced we have so little. Nothing short of a conversion would do.

A minister worked as an interim pastor of a church where people are accustomed to doing the same thing every week. The members of that church have a lot of customs and traditions, and they don't like anybody disrupting them. One custom has been to put a loaf of bread on the communion plate every week.

They do not celebrate the Lord's Supper every week, but they have a symbol of the sacrament. If you think that would be expensive or wasteful to have an unused loaf of bread on the communion table every week, don't worry. They use the same loaf. It is a large unsliced loaf of Italian bread covered with polyurethane. So they use the same bread over and over again. One Sunday my friend was leading the people in communion. He lifted the ceremonial loaf of bread, said, "Take, eat, this is my body." Then he cracked it open and ripped it apart.

There was a collective gasp in the congregation. Then it was absolutely silent as he continued to break the bread into large chunks to place on the communion trays. It took a few minutes for people to realize my friend had switched the polyurethane bread with a real loaf.

Afterward someone said, "You really had us going there for a minute. We actually thought you broke our communion bread."

The minister said, "Don't you understand? If it is not broken, it cannot be shared."

Fearful, But Not Afraid

This is a frightening story, but not merely because it reveals that Jesus walked on water. I have a profound respect for the Christ, tempered by years of Sunday school and Bible study. He is the Lord, the Son of God, the one through whom all things are made. As such, he could sidestep his own laws of physics. You might doubt this, but I do not.

No, it is not the mysterious power and presence of Jesus that scares me. It is his invitation to get out of the boat and step onto the sea. He said to Peter, "Come." On behalf of all who would follow Jesus, Peter stepped out of the boat and onto the surface of the water.

Peter meant well. He wanted to affirm it was the Lord and not a specter in the dark, so he suggested a bargain with Jesus. "If it truly is you," he hollered into the wind, "tell me to step onto the sea." That is exactly what Jesus did.

But then things began to sink. Peter was profoundly frightened, says the gospel of Matthew. He kept his eyes focused on the Lord until the fierce wind slapped him in the face. He descended into the water and cried out for help. That is how I know the story is true. Peter, the star disciple, was afraid. I can understand that. Fear rises up in the soul at the most inopportune time.

Say, for instance, you enter a room full of new faces. The air is charged with the buzz of multiple conversations. Laughter dances in the air. Everybody is having a good time and you don't know a single person. Even though you may be a gregarious and outgoing soul, an occasion like that can stir up fear.

Or what if you are enlisted to speak to a crowd? The first time I ever gave a speech, three hundred high school classmates spread out in long rows before me. The families of all the graduates sat behind them, filling up our football stadium. When I stepped up to the podium, I took in that view and gasped. As I looked down at my one page speech, carefully edited by the vice principal and filled with adolescent platitudes, every word on the page had its hand in the air, begging, "May I be excused?" Public speaking can be a fearsome moment, perhaps the most terrifying of all.

Different things evoke fear in each of us. Backpacking in the wilderness? I've been there and done that. Walking along a mountain rim with two thousand feet of open air to my immediate left? Ah, I did that as a fourteen-year-old Boy Scout. Confronting a black bear who broke into your stash of backpacking food? We banged on tin pots with metal spoons, sent him scurrying away, and only later considered how dangerous that was. But zip-lining or bungee jumping - no thanks, I will not do either. All of us have an invisible line we will not cross.

What about the invitation to step out onto the sea? There is no life preserver, nothing beneath the feet, no convenient rock to step upon. What a frightening invitation!

Deep water is terrifying. In the scriptures, the sea takes on mythic proportions. The psalmist cried out in the day of trouble, "Save me, O God, for the waters have come up to my neck. I have come into deep waters, and the flood sweeps over me."(Psalm 69:1, 3) This is the experience of the beginning swimmer, the passenger in the swamped boat, or those who are in over their heads.

In the day of Jesus, it was widely perceived that the sea was the abode of demons. Remember the story of Jesus encountering the demon-possessed man who lived in a graveyard? The legion of unclean spirits inside the ill man begged the Lord not to send them "back into the abyss."[26] Jesus did it anyway, casting the demons into a group of unclean pigs, who dashed down the embankment and drowned in the sea. It was believed the deep water was a portal to hell.

That's why a sudden storm could whip up and threaten somebody's life, especially at night. Every experienced fisherman knew this, including Simon Peter. Yet Jesus said to him, "Come, step out on the water."

It was an invitation for Peter to confront his fears, even for the fisherman who had spent most of his adult lifetime on the water. By inviting him to get out of the boat, to step on the water, Jesus was pressing him to answer the question, "What are you afraid of?"

Chances are, if pressed, we might be afraid of many things: afraid of what tomorrow will bring, afraid that the past may catch up to us, or afraid of what might lurk in the dark shadows today. We could take a few moments today to list our fears, whether they are real terrors or imaginative anxieties. If we step onto the water, we will reveal who we are.

In Peter May's novel, *The Black House*, a teenage boy was invited on a hunting trip upon a small island off the coast of Scotland. He didn't want to go. It threatened to be dangerous.

The leader of the trip confronted him by saying, "Whatever your blackest fear. Whatever your greatest weakness. These are things you must face up to. Things you must confront, or you'll spend the rest of your life regretting it."[27]

So, Peter looked into the eyes of Jesus and stepped out onto the water. For the moment, it worked. Christ invited him to do something that he was able to do: Simon Peter could step onto the sea. He could do this, he has this... until he started to sink.

It was a darkly comical moment, or at least it strikes me that way. Anybody who has suspended disbelief for this long has known that a 185-pound Galilean fisherman could not stand upon a large body of water. He would sink, and would always sink. Any scientist with a third grade education would say this.

But this was not a scientific story. This was a faith story and therefore it was a deeply soulful story. When the Bible sings praises of God, it declares it is God "alone who stretched out the heavens and trampled the waves of the sea."(Job 9:8) Isaiah said the Lord, "makes a way in the sea, a path in the mighty waters."(Isaiah 43:16) So today's story from the gospel of Matthew is more than a miracle story; it is an affirmation that the Christ of God is stronger than the demons of the deep. He walked over them and invited Peter - and the rest of us - to step out with him. This was an incredible affirmation ... until Peter began to sink.

Not only does the story reveal who Jesus was, it reveals who Peter was, who all of us are. Try as we might, there are some fears we cannot overcome, giants we cannot slay, and situations that we cannot quite overcome, at least not yet. There are situations of physics and fluid dynamics that we cannot overcome, just as there are matters of the heart that threaten and terrify.

Peter cried out, "Lord, save me." The Lord extended his hand and rescued him. This was a good reminder that at the heart of all we can find truth and hope. At the point of our extremity, there is a savior who grabs our hand to rescue.

But our real hope is this: after the moment comes when we've been tested, after we stand nose to nose with our terror, the Christ who walked upon the waves also got into the boat with us. As the angel declared before his birth, Jesus is Emmanuel, "God with us."(Matthew 1:23) As the risen Lord said on the mountain top, "I am with you always, even to the end."(Matthew 28:20)

Years ago, a mission team from our congregation went to Haiti to learn more about a literacy clinic that our church was supporting. It was a challenging trip, and our volunteers were stretched emotionally and physically. At the end, they purchased a wood carving as a gift for the leader who had inspired the trip. It portrayed Jesus with his arms around the twelve disciples, all of them portrayed by the artist in various stages of anxiety and disbelief. His arms and shoulders formed the rim of what became a fishing vessel. The artist declared, "It is a perfect image for the church: we are the people who are in the same boat with Jesus." Indeed.

Whatever fears we face, we are together, and can choose to look to one another for support and encouragement. None of us have to face fears alone. We are companions floating together above destruction and its terroristic demands.

And we are together with Jesus. We don't choose this, for he decides to get in the boat with his people. It is because he is with us that we can address the fears that threaten to immobilize us. Humiliation and embarrassment? He has come through them, and he is with us. Abandonment and loneliness? He has come through them too, and he is still with us. The dark specter of death? The fear that God has abandoned us? The risen Christ has moved through the most fearsome night, has the scars to prove it... and he climbs into our boat again and again.

When I was a teenager, I was fortunate to have a pastor who taught me this lesson, not merely with words but with the trust of his heart. He was a young father, at home one evening with three small children. There was a knock at the door, and he answered it. A state policeman stood there, holding his hat, and said, "Sir, I regret to inform you that your wife was killed in a car accident." The news was devastating.

In time, he remarried and the children grew. His oldest son went to school to get his pilot's license. He and his wife had a baby girl, with another child on the way. He put in his flight time, got a job at a small airport, and began to run air freight throughout the southern states. He hoped to become a missionary pilot some day.

One night, the son was flying and there was an engine failure. In a rough landing, the gas tank exploded, and he never had a chance. Once again, the news was devastating. What do you do when your life goes to pieces again?

My pastor said, "The grief, twice over, was terribly hard work. But coming through it all, I came to believe that the most powerful word of Jesus is this: fear not." He reminded us that this is the first word of the Christmas angel, the first word on Easter, and the final gospel invitation for all of us. Don't be afraid!

I do not know all the challenges you face. I do not know the burdens you carry. I cannot presume to know what fears are nipping at your heels. But I do know this: Christ is greater than our fears and he walks upon the waves. If we see him, the sheer power of his authority might, in its own way, be overwhelming to us. But we never have to be afraid. He is with us, even to the end of the age.

Proper 15 / Ordinary Time 20

Matthew 15:21-28

Love And Boundaries

Let's face it. This story is difficult to understand. I have been struggling with it all week. But then I heard a short phrase that offered some help. I am not sure if the phrase came to me in a dream or a conversation. I cannot recall if I heard in a Top 40 tune or a country and western song. Nevertheless the phrase has given me an angle to understand this text. The phrase is "love with boundaries." Have you ever heard those words? Have you ever used them yourself? Before I read this story, it never occurred to me that perhaps the love of Jesus had boundaries.

At least, that is how the story began. Here was a woman whose daughter was tormented by a demon. We do not know the specific details. Perhaps she saw her child awaken each morning with twisted limbs beneath her. Or maybe she watched under the hot noonday sun as her daughter dropped clean laundry in the dust and placed fingers on a throbbing head. Perhaps it happened after the moon came out and the mother's peaceful sleep was pierced by her daughter's screams. We don't know the details of the situation. But we do know the woman had a problem. Her daughter's pain was brought on by forces outside her control. And did you notice the story? Jesus seemed reluctant to heal her daughter. Why didn't Jesus help? Did his love have boundaries?

If so, that might strike us as strange. The mother's request sounded like a hundred other requests. Plenty of people asked Jesus for help and healing. Once a leper said, "Lord, if you choose, you can make me clean." Jesus touched him, saying, "I do choose. Be made clean!" Immediately the leper was healed. Jesus made him well. Not long after that, Matthew said, "They brought to Jesus many who were possessed by demons; and he cast out the spirits with a word, and he healed all who were sick." The storyteller added, "This was to fulfill what was spoken by the prophet Isaiah, `He took our infirmities. He carried our diseases.'"(Matthew 8:14-17) Jesus came to touch the sick and bear human pain.

Why didn't Jesus instantly heal that woman's daughter? Did his love have boundaries?

That would be unusual, especially since the woman took the matter so seriously. She came with all the right words on her lips. Did you notice that? Sometimes people are embarrassed to talk about their problems, but not her. She said, "A demon torments my daughter." Sometimes people don't know what they should ask for in time of trouble, but she said, "Have mercy on me!" Sometimes people are too proud to ask others for assistance. Yet this woman had the courage to say, "Help me!" She spoke all the correct words.

Yet Jesus stood in silence. Why didn't Jesus snap his fingers and heal that woman's daughter? Did his love have boundaries?

After all, the Canaanite woman knew to whom she spoke. She called him both "Lord" and "Son of David." In Matthew's gospel, those are the two basic confessions of faith. Jesus is the Son of David, the Messiah who delivers us from evil. Three times in this passage, she calls Jesus "Lord", the one with all authority over heaven and earth." Her insight was remarkable. Thus far in this gospel, Jesus' own disciples have not learned such theologically sound faith. Neither have they put their theology into liturgical practice. The text says the woman literally "worshiped" Jesus. Her uncommon insights bent her knees in prayer. She knew right doctrine and knelt in right worship.

So why didn't Jesus heal her daughter? Did his love have boundaries?

Was it because she was a native of a foreign country? I hate to bring this up, but the gospel of Matthew seems inclined to keep her nationality before us. Matthew calls her a "Canaanite woman." When Mark told the story, he merely called her "a woman." But Matthew insisted, "She was a Canaanite." That word Canaanite is an old word. An angry word. A bitter word. When the Jews came to the promised land, they drove out the Canaanites. For years, the Jews kept the Canaanites up north, near the Mediterranean, and wiping out more than a few along the way. They pushed the Canaanites to the other side of the border. The Jewish law said, "Keep it that way. Don't mix with the Canaanites."(Deuteronomy 20:17-18) Certainly Jesus the Jew knew that law.

What's more, the gospel of Matthew claimed that Jesus twice said, "My only business is finding lost Jews."(Matthew 10:6, 15:24) That suggests Jesus may have had borders he was unwilling to cross. Was this the reason why Jesus was reluctant to heal the woman's daughter? Did his love have boundaries?

Of course, it may disturb us to think about Jesus in such a way, even though we have probably met religious people who make such distinctions. I know a clergy person of another church who is very proud of his record in helping the poor. He said, "Whenever they knock on my door and request a handout, I always ask them the same question. I ask, `You're not a member of my church, are you?' If they are not members of my church, I will not help them." You see, they stand beyond his boundaries.

I don't know how you feel about that. But it is true that some people erect fences around their love. They say things like:

> "I can't kiss her, she's black."
> "I can't hug him, he's gay."
> "I can't hire her, she's Hispanic."
> "I can't marry him, he's disabled."
> "I can't trust her, she's unfaithful."
> "I can't turn my back on him, he's Vietnamese."
> Or perhaps, "I can't help her, she's a Canaanite."

Don't forget - Jesus stood on Canaanite soil. He was a traveler in a foreign land. You know how that is. Even if we move across the border into another country, sometimes we carry our boundaries with us.

Have you ever been on the tour bus in a foreign land? There you are, in air conditioned comfort, looking out the window at the people who live there. It can be tempting to compare their lives to your own. Sadly, some of us have overheard the comments, some of them deprecating, some of them downright racist. The sad truth is the commentary reveals more about the commentators than it does about those who are observed.

During one awkward trip, I began to wonder why an outspoken tourist had not stayed home, especially if he could not refrain from putting down the people of that land and their living conditions. The uncomfortable truth is that he had never really left home. He brought "home" with him, with all of its biases and boundaries.

Get the picture: here stood Jesus the Jew on Canaanite soil and a native woman came up and said, "Lord, Son of David, have mercy on me!" Jesus stood there, not saying a word, and the woman kept begging for help.

The disciples said, "Jesus, can't you get rid of her?" Yet the woman kept begging for help.

Jesus said, "Excuse me, lady, but I came only to seek lost Jews." Still the woman begged for help.

Jesus said, "It's not fair to throw my good bread to the dogs." But the woman kept begging for help. *She would not let him go.*

Then she said, "If you are talking about what's fair, is it fair for so-called dogs like me to go hungry?"

With that, I think we can picture Jesus standing there, his jaw hanging open. For a second time he did not know what to say, he was so amazed at that woman's faith, a faith which beckoned his love beyond Jewish boundaries. When Jesus found his voice, of course, he healed that woman's daughter. Even with her daughter out of sight, even though he would probably never meet the Canaanite girl, even though it was against the ancient law from

Deuteronomy, Jesus healed the woman's daughter. And do you know why? Because love, true love, moves beyond all boundaries.

The Christian disciple can affirm this, even though it may continue to be a struggle for many people. We are the children of our circumstances. Perhaps we were born without prejudice, but we pick up prejudice rather quickly. Maybe our families were open minded and open hearted, at least at the beginning, yet there may have been episodes along the way that began to put epithets and judgments into the air.

We know from the New Testament that the earliest circles of Christian believers struggled too, particularly as the gospel moved beyond the original circle of Jewish followers of Jesus. The most significant debate in the New Testament was over the question of whether the church would admit Gentiles into the membership. The struggle was real, the change came slowly.

Whether it was an Italian soldier knocking at Simon Peter's door, the Macedonians welcoming the apostle Paul, or the first council at Jerusalem,[28] the earliest followers of Jesus wrestled with the extent to which the gospel could be preached and outsiders could be welcomed. It was resolved only when the Christians perceived that God pushes the church beyond its own borders. These days, we can only move beyond our own discrimination and racism if we can see that this is the ongoing mission of God: to welcome all in the name of Christ.

Taken by itself, the story of Jesus and the Canaanite woman is troubling. It offers a brief glimpse of old-fashioned provincialism, an ugly picture of people divided by ethnic distinctions. Yet it is merely a snapshot of the movement at its beginning. As Christians, we remember the rest of the story that Christ came for all people without distinction or restriction. In love with the whole world, Jesus stretched out his arms to save all people, both Jews and Canaanites, pilgrims and pagans. Three days later, the risen Lord gathered people on a mountain and said, "Authority beyond all boundaries has been given to me. Go and spread God's love to everybody. Make disciples from every kind of people under heaven" (Matthew 28:16-20).

Ever since that moment, we have known what to do. We have known whom to embrace. For the rest of the gospel is clear: true love has no boundaries, because on the cross Christ our true lover has stretched out his arms to embrace strangers of every nation. His love determines our mission.

Wherever The Messiah Is

When you were a little kid, did you have a favorite super hero? The kind of super hero that you could read about in the comic books?

Batman was pretty cool, sticking to the shadows of night but full of ingenuity and agility. He had all those nifty gadgets in his utility belt! Or there was The Flash, who could run faster than the speed of light. Or the Incredible Hulk with his radioactive strength. Of course, the favorite for a lot of us was Superman. Faster than a speeding locomotive, he could leap tall buildings in a single bound and catch bullets in his hand.

Like most little kids, I spent a lot of time daydreaming about those super powers. If only there was some special ability that would make us stand out or lift us above the pack. A lot of kids dream about that.

One of my daughters was enchanted by Harry Potter. When she was little, she would have loved to wave the magic wand to change back the clock, alter nature, cast a spell, clean her bedroom, or direct some zombies to do her math homework. Unfortunately she didn't have the ability. No super powers!

When you're a kid, a super hero offers the possibility of transcending circumstances and limitations. If you had the super power, you could say to the wind, "Be still," and it would be still. You could say to the stones, "Become bread," and there would be plenty of food for the multitude to eat. I suppose you could even walk on water!

No wonder, then, that a kid like me could hear the stories of Jesus and be drawn to him. The Bible stories about Jesus revealed someone of great power and authority. That's the gospel of Mathew's favorite word: "authority." Three different times, Matthew said Jesus had the authority to heal every single sick person (4:23, 8:16, 9:35). Every one!

Jesus also had extraordinary power in his words. He could speak truth to the Pharisees and scribes, and make them quiver in their boots. He could speak mercy and restoration to the leper who had been cast out of town. He could speak forgiveness and healing to the one who was paralyzed.

Jesus was unusual. If you didn't know better, you might think he can from the planet Krypton.

I can understand why Simon Peter had a hard time making sense out of him. Not only did Jesus have the power, but sometimes when he spoke, it sounded like jibberish. Some of his words didn't make sense. This man who seemed to have amazing power said to Peter, "I am going to the cross. I must give my life. I must hand over everything and sacrifice my life." And Peter said, "That is nonsense. It's never going to happen to you. Not you, of all people."

Jesus responded, "Get behind me. You see things only from a human point of view, not a holy point of view." You are saying that from the perspective of a little kid who wishes he had super powers. You assume that advancement is the key to all of life. You are thinking beyond a first-century peasant who lives under constant occupation by a hostile military power. And it is extremely confusing.

It was confusing for many in that first circle of disciples. If Jesus is the Messiah, what would he be doing on a cross? The Messiah was going to come and get rid of all the crosses. That was the first-century assumption for many. They believed the Messiah would ride into town on a gleaming white horse. He would wear a pure white robe, he would be morally unstained, he would stand taller and stronger than anybody we know.

That meant he would redeem Israel out of a thousand years of degradation. They have been kicked around by all the other nations, and the Messiah would make things right. He was going to restore the kingdom. He would fix what didn't work. He would drive out the people from other nations. He was going to make Israel great again! That is what they wanted in a Messiah.

Whatever they needed, that's what they wanted. Whatever they wanted, that's what they expected. So why was Jesus talking about a cross?

No wonder most of Jesus' followers dwindled away after Jesus was arrested and condemned. He did not look strong and mighty. So much for all his super powers.

Yet here is the truth, the upside down truth: that Jesus was not only the Messiah, but that his super power was something called *kenosis*. That is the New Testament word for it. *Kenosis* is the word from one of Paul's letters. It means "to empty oneself," to "lose oneself," to "give one's self away." Jesus set aside the glory that was rightfully his own and took up the mantle of a servant.

This is hard for us to swallow, and difficult for us to understand.

A number of years ago, my friend Jane was being examined by the presbytery as the final step before she could be ordained as a preacher. Some of you might have been there. The meeting was up at a church camp in the woods. They asked her all kinds of questions. One old duffer, a minister well known for his grandstanding said, "Jane, tell us why Christianity is superior to all other religions."

Jane looked at him and asked him to repeat the question. "Jane, why is Christianity superior to all other religions?" That prompted me to think about it as well. It is the kind of question that tells you much more about the questioner than the one being questioned.

Jane was good on her feet. Like a good rabbi, she questioned the question: "Why do you think we are superior? What happens to others if we start declaring we are superior?"

Meanwhile, I thought about how I would answer the question. One answer seemed to come to me, as if a light went on. If I were to answer how Christian faith is superior to all other expressions of faith, I think I would say its superiority is in its humility. True Christian faith is shaped like Jesus, who set aside all the glory and took on the mantle of a servant, even to the point of death on a cross.

It is hard to understand this. Jesus says the only way to understand it is through an experience of revelation, through an "aha moment" which comes as a gift from God's Holy Spirit. That nobody can apprehend this truth unless the Spirit comes and breathes it anew, so that mind and heart can understand what is not obvious. Otherwise it will not make any sense to those with any power or privilege.

In the recurring moments through history when the church has been intoxicated with its own sense of power or privilege, it doesn't understand – much less follow – the Christ who gives up everything for the life of the world.

For this is the truth at the heart of it all: once we used to say, "When the Messiah comes, there will be no more misery," but now we affirm, "wherever there is misery, there is the Messiah."[29]

Try to let that sink in for a little bit, if you can. That's the hidden truth at the heart of our faith. It's not about being superior, but about becoming available. It's not about being first, but humbly choosing to be last. It is not about being right, but about being so completely humane that you shine like the sun in holiness.

Henri Nouwen wrote a book some years ago, based on a few talks about the move of setting aside all glory for the sake of becoming deeply human and thus holy. The title says it all: *The Downward Mobility of Christ.* Christian growth is not about advancing, but emptying. It's not about jangling the keys to the kingdom as if they are your accomplishment or your private possession, but rather about unlocking the prisoners and setting them free to experience the deep love of God ... which is precisely what Jesus is all about.

What would that look like, as a model for you or me? How might the followers of Jesus become more like him?

A woman who runs an after-school tutoring program was talking about her volunteers. It's a pretty effective program. Kids stop by after school, before the parents pick them up after work. There's a snack, and a few minutes of fun. As you would expect, the core of the program is a group of concerned volunteers.

She said they come in two kinds. The first group of volunteers has great concern for the kids. They exude expertise and years of experience. "Sit down, kids, and let me show you how it's done. Let's straighten out your nouns and verbs. Let's make sure all your numbers add up. I will be the expert and tell you what to do."

But the second group of volunteers, a much smaller group, takes a different approach. They don't tell the kids to sit down; they go and sit with them. They learn their names. They never claim to be experts. They ask a lot of questions: where are you struggling? What don't you understand? What would you like me to show you? Then they just sit there and listen. They set their pre-conceived agendas aside and let the kids do the talking.

"I am grateful for all of my volunteers," said the director, "but I've noticed that the second group is more effective over time. They come alongside the kids and try to understand the world as the kids experience it. They actually change the kids for the better."

Simon Peter didn't completely understand this. He knew Jesus was special, that he was different somehow. He saw the healings, the miracles, and the astounding abilities. All he could perceive was the Lord's power. But his insight went only halfway. What he didn't yet understand is that the true power of the Christ (the superpower, if you will) is his humility, his setting aside the glory for the sake of serving others, his compassion, his willingness to come alongside us – and all others who need him.

Simon Peter figured out that the Messiah had come, and it was Jesus. The Spirit of God opened his mind just wide enough that he could perceive that. But he didn't yet realize the whole truth of the gospel: that the Messiah, the Christ, came to us ... not to fish us out of our humanity, but to inhabit it with us. For that is the promise that opens and concludes the gospel of Matthew: Jesus is God-with-us always, even to the end of the age (1:23, 28:20).

- There is nowhere so dark that the light of Christ is not present.
- There is no place of suffering that the Messiah cannot enter.
- There is no cross that we carry that he has not carried already.
- There is no tomb so desolate and absent that Jesus will be shut out or shut in.
- He is with us. *Always.*

This is the will of God, the divine gift, the gospel truth that we are known and we are found because we are loved. That's good news.

The Messiah is here, and it is Jesus. As someone has said, "The first task of a Messiah is to get people to stop looking for one."[30]

Proper 17 / Ordinary Time 22

Matthew 16:21-28

Revising The Agenda

Whenever I hear this Bible passage, I smell potato soup. One day when I was about fourteen years old, my mother announced we were going to church for something called a "sacrificial" supper. She said it had something to do with the season of Lent. That was curious, too. We were a low-church Presbyterian family. Liturgical seasons didn't mean much to us. Any talk of Lent didn't make much sense. At least, not until that night.

There we were, one Sunday night in late winter. The fellowship hall was half-empty. We sat at tables and waited to be served a great banquet. When the kitchen door finally opened, somebody brought out a pot of potato soup. It was white and pasty. It smelled like onions. I pushed my bowl aside and waited for the next course, which never arrived. It seemed like a cruel joke. The entire menu for the dinner was potato soup. There was nothing else to eat.

At the end of dinner, our minister stood up and explained we were doing this because it was Lent and Lent is the season of self-denial. On a normal Sunday, he said, we might be sitting down to a large meal, but this particular night we were giving up a fine dinner and choosing a simpler menu. Our minister also said the reason we were doing this was because Christians are people who deny themselves, pick up a cross, and follow Jesus.

To this day I cannot understand what potato soup had to do with Christian discipleship, but the association remains fixed in my brain.

When we hear this scripture passage, it is as if we are returned to the season of Lent. That is the traditional time of preparation, a season to move toward the cross and prepare ourselves for the resurrection. There's no question that self-denial is a central theme for such days, which often coincide with a bleak North American winter.

But when we probe deeper, we hear that self-denial is central to the story of Jesus. It is a central theme in the passage we heard a few minutes ago. Jesus told his disciples he was going to suffer and die. This was the first time he said it. Here in a central text of the gospel of Matthew, the secret was out - that Jesus who saves will suffer. The one who confronts every kind of evil will be destroyed by evil. Jesus will deny himself and pick up a cross. He chose to save the world, even if it meant losing his life.

Simon Peter didn't understand this and, frankly, who can blame him? It's a difficult message to hear. If anybody wants help from Jesus, they must remember how he endured suffering and rejection. Jesus did not swoop down from heaven ready to snatch us from the earth. Rather, he came down to earth and stayed here until he was buried in the ground. Immediately before our text, Peter made his great confession: "Jesus, you're the Messiah." And he was right.

What Peter could not comprehend was that Jesus gave his life as an act of self-denial. He took the low road all the way to the cross. That is a hard picture to keep in focus. His sacrifice judges our perceptions of success and accomplishment.

But the word that is even more difficult to hear is the word Jesus says to all of us. "If any want to be my followers, let them deny themselves and take up the cross and follow me." The low road Jesus took is the only road available for anyone who tags along behind him. This is not an easy word for us to hear.

The three imperatives clang like a cracked bell: deny yourself, take up your cross, follow me. What are we going to do about this?

It is particularly difficult because we often take these words to mean that we should put ourselves down for the sake of the gospel, that we should deprive ourselves to the glory of God, even to the point of denying our God-given dignity. In my experience, the people who get most upset about this point of view are smart, capable women, and with good reason. Historically, a lot of women have been subject to a systematic put-down. They have been told they are second-class citizens, that they are expected to serve everybody else.

A friend went to pay a call on a wealthy rancher in another state. He went on behalf of the college where he worked. The development office set up the appointment in the hope that this rancher might give some money for a scholarship to the college. My friend traveled out there, he knocked on the door and was shown inside. As they began to chat, he realized he and the rancher were not alone. A woman in a gray shawl shuffled quietly through the back of the room. The rancher said, "Bring our guest something to eat!" She shuffled in and set some food before them without saying a word. The men continued to talk.

The rancher said, "Come and get his dishes." The woman in gray shuffled in, collected the plates, never making eye contact, and she left. The conversation between the men ended.

The rancher said, "Bring his coat!" She shuffled in with his coat and then quickly disappeared. He was halfway home on his flight when the man from the college said, "I just can't deal with this."

He got home and couldn't sleep all night. As he confessed, "I wanted to go back there, look her in the eye, thank her for all her kindness, and give some humanity back to her."

Jesus said, "Deny yourselves." You know, it's difficult for some people to even hear that word when they've had so much taken away. How can people in poverty believe it is a virtue to give up what little dignity they bear? How can the downtrodden ever hear this obligation of the gospel?

Sometimes we need to claim the love and dignity of God and then see what happens. Like the woman who made an appointment to talk about troubles at home. At one point in our conversation she said, "When my opinion of myself improved, my marriage got worse."

For those who struggle to feel empowered, for those who believe for the first time in their lives they are worthy of love and appreciation, it can be harsh to hear Jesus say, "Deny yourself." It's particularly true if you have recently discovered that you have a self.

Today I want to suggest that the best way to hear these words is to hear them within the entire context of Matthew's gospel. According to Matthew, Jesus came to make a constructive difference in the world. Jesus came to confront every force that disturbs and destroys human life. Throughout this gospel he is sent by God to give back dignity to all who have it taken away. Picture the leper who was segregated from the community by his disease. Jesus restored him to health and community. See the woman who lived on the fringe of town suffering from a hemorrhage -- Jesus healed her and gave her a name. Look at the sinner who could not undo the effects of his misdeeds -- Jesus canceled all his debts with God.

Listen: Matthew told us how Jesus came to give worth and value, not take it away.

I have begun to think and rethink the order of those three imperatives: deny yourself, carry a cross, follow me.

Which comes first? Which is most important to God? We can deny ourselves, but as we know, we run the risk of ignoring our God-given dignity. We can go out looking for crosses to carry, and I'm sure you realize there are people who love to do that, always looking for a cause to annoy somebody else, always dressing in the armor of a martyr, always saying, "Hit me again." There are some people who are never happy unless they are suffering in some way, and they get so smug about it.

The point is, Jesus never said, "Go out into the world and get yourself beaten up!" But he did say, "Follow me." In my reading of the gospel of Matthew, that's what matters. We are invited to follow Jesus. We are called for and called upon to follow him. His invitation comes before every other claim on our lives.

Following Jesus means two things. First, we become his disciples. That means we put ourselves in the position to learn from him. We give up the allusion that we are experts in leading our own lives. We revise our personal agendas and we learn from Jesus.

Second, if we follow Jesus, that means we will engage in the same work that Jesus has been doing, which is to say we will speak out against every mean spirit, we will feed the hungry and heal the sick, we will speak the truth, we will touch the untouchable, forgive the unforgivable and love the unlovable. We will do God's work in the world, just like Jesus. When we do that, we have every reason to expect that what happened to him might happen to us.

"As one New Testament scholar reminds us, the members of the early church were not called to suffer. They were called to preach the gospel. Because of the confrontational nature of that calling, the world they confront will persecute them in order to stop them. Suffering is the result of the call, not the call itself. What happened to Jesus, for the same reason it happened to him, will happen to those acting and preaching in his name."[31]

Friends, we don't wake up every morning and say, "How am I going to let the world beat me up today?" But we are called upon to get out of bed to ask, "How can I let the whole world know the life of Jesus is the hope of the world?"

Once I thought those three commands had to stay in the same order as they appear in the Bible: Deny yourself, go looking for a cross, and then follow Jesus. But the more I reflect on this the more I realize the emphasis moves in the other direction. The most important thing we can ever do is to follow Jesus Christ, to learn from him and to do his work. Then if the world hands us a cross, we shouldn't expect anything different.

Jesus says, "Come, follow me." That does not mean we will intentionally put ourselves in positions where we will be put down, beaten up, or killed. But it does mean we will take God more seriously than we take ourselves.

In one of his books, John Calvin said that self-denial is "the sum of the Christian life."[32] He claimed that it is the heart of true piety, the basis of generous stewardship, and the source of our helpfulness to our neighbors. Denying ourselves in this context means we hold back because we have put God's purposes before our own. It's the kind of spiritual discipline, says Calvin, that "erases from our minds the yearning to possess, the desire for power, and the desire for the favor of others." True self-denial "uproots ambition and all craving for human glory." Why? Because it means we choose to put God's ways before our own pursuits. We choose to follow Jesus and to do his work. And nothing else will ever come before it.

"Follow me. Pick up your cross. Deny yourself." Whether we hear these days in the winter of Lent or the dog days of summer, this is Christ's invitation. It never means that we give up our dignity, but it does mean that we will take on the mantle of faithfulness. We will speak as Jesus spoke. We will act as Jesus came to act. And if a cross is given to us, we will not carry it alone - for Jesus Christ is risen from the dead.

Endnotes

1   Neill Q. Hamilton, *Maturing in the Christian Life: A Pastor's Guide* (Philadelphia: The Geneva Press, 1984) 69.

2   Raymond E. Brown, *A Risen Christ in Eastertime* (Collegeville MN: The Liturgical Press, 1991) 75.

3   As quoted in "The Easter Texts," Kimberly Clayton, *Journal for Preachers*, Easter 2007, pp. 5-6.

4   Attributed to Lewis Smedes, exact source unknown.

5   Dr. Craddock, the great preacher, said this line many times.

6   Thanks to Dr. Craig Barnes, president of Princeton Theological Seminary, for sharing these insights from an unpublished manuscript.

7   James H. Smylie, Dean K. Thompson, and Cary Patrick, Go Therefore: 150 Years of Presbyterians in Global Mission, ed. Cary Patrick (Atlanta: Presbyterian Publishing House, 1987) v.

8   Douglas John Hall, unpublished lecture.

9   Eugene H. Peterson, *The Message* (Colorado Springs: NavPress, 2003)

10 Source unknown.

11 Frederick Buechner, *Whistling in the Dark: An ABC Theologized* (San Francisco: Harper & Row, Publishers, 1988) 4-5.

12 Joseph Fitzmyer, *The Gospel of Luke: The Anchor Bible* (New York: Doubleday, 1981) 848.

13 As told in Walter Wangerin, Jr., *Ragman and Other Cries of Faith* (San Francisco: Harper & Row, Publishers, 1984) 62-64.

14 Ronald C. White, Jr., Liberty and Justice for All: Radical Reform and the Social Gospel (San Francisco: Harper & Row, Publishers, 1990) p. 131.

15 Elizabeth Leland, "Black church, white neighbors," The Charlotte Observer, 28 August 2009.

16 Henri J. M Nouwen, *Reaching Out: The Three Movements of the Spiritual Life* (New York: Image Books, 1975) p. 71.

17 Ibid, p. 76

18 Rule of Saint Benedict, chapter 53. Available online at http://www.osb.org/rb/text/toc.html

19 Wayne Muller, *Sabbath* (New York: Bantam, 1999) 51-52

20 Wendell Berry, *This Day: Collected and New Sabbath Poems* (Berkeley: Counterpoint Press, 2013), introduction.

21 David Brooks, "Obama, Gospel and Verse," The New York Times, 26 April 2007, A 25.

22   A true vignette, borrowed from another preacher, who probably borrowed from somebody else.

23   Frederick Buechner, *Wishful Thinking* (New York: Harper and Row)

24   As quoted in Elizabeth O Connor, Letters to Scattered Pilgrims (San Francisco: Harper and Row, Publishers, 1979) 17-18.

25   These statistics were taken from the interpretive materials for the One Great Hour of Sharing, a special offering in which the Presbyterian Church (USA) participates.

26   See the version of the exorcism as told in Luke 8:31.

27   Peter May, The Black House (London: Quercus, 2014) 207.

28   See, for instance, Acts 10:1-48, Acts 16:6-40, and Acts 15:1-41.

29   Fred Craddock first said this so well, and so clearly. See his sermon "Hoping or Postponing," originally recorded on the National Radio Pulpit in 1978.

30   Thanks, Fred Craddock. Op. cit.

31   Brian K. Blount, "Preaching the Kingdom: Mark's Apocalyptic Call for Prophetic Engagement," *The Princeton Seminary Bulletin*, 1994. p. 55.

32   John Calvin, *Institutes of the Christian Religion*, Book III, Chapter VII, "The Sum of the Christian Life: The Denial of Ourselves," ed. John T. McNeill (Philadelphia: The Westminster Press, 1960) pp. 689-701.

www.ingramcontent.com/pod-product-compliance
Lightning Source LLC
Chambersburg PA
CBHW022027090426
42739CB00006BA/320